MW01252270

MEDITERRANEAN
SLOW
COOKER

101

Best of Easy and Delicious Mediterranean Slow Cooker Recipes
to a Healthy Life

J. J. Lewis

Want more Bestseller Cook Books for **FREE?**

Join my **V.I.P** Reading List where I give away **Healthy** and Delicious Recipes **FOR FREE!**

Yes, you heard me right! COMPLETELY FREE to everyone just for being a loyal reader of mine!

www.ravenspress.com/jjlewis

RAVENS|PRESS

Copyright © 2015 by Ravens Press
All rights reserved. This book or any portion thereof
may not be reproduced or used in any manner whatsoever
without the express written permission of the publisher
except for the use of brief quotations in a book review.

ISBN-13: 978-1508598626

ISBN-10: 1508598622

www.amazon.com/author/jjlewis

Table of Contents

INTRODUCTION

Fresh fish, clean flavors and lots of vibrant vegetables define Mediterranean dishes. Cretans ate in a way that hadn't much changed since ancient times. Their meals were full of vegetables and fruits, abundant in beans and fish, and almost devoid of red meat and processed foods. They regularly took in high amounts of fat — 40 percent of daily calories — but most of it came from olive oil; their average saturated-fat intake was among the world's lowest. This eating pattern was soon christened the "Mediterranean Diet," and it still stands as one of the world's healthiest, tastiest ways to eat. Eating foods from the Mediterranean diet is an easy way to improve your health—those who follow the diet are less likely to develop high blood pressure, high cholesterol or become obese. These low-calorie recipes from the Mediterranean are a delicious way to eat healthfully. A dish of sautéed polenta, beans and spinach take its inspiration from the Catalan region of Spain. A slow-cooker recipe for chicken and vegetables is full of Greek flavors. These are some healthy inspiration to your meals which are low in calories. A hallmark of Mediterranean dishes is that they derive deep flavor from simple ingredients prepared simply

CONTENT

Rich in culture and food history, the nations on the shores of the brilliant azure Mediterranean Sea—Italy, Spain, France, Morocco, Greece, Lebanon, Syria, Turkey and Israel—have all contributed something special to the colorful, vibrant tapestry that is Mediterranean cuisine. Key components of Mediterranean cuisine include heart-healthy olive oil, protein-rich legumes, fish and whole grains with moderate amounts of wine and red meat. The flavors are rich, and the health benefits for people choosing a Mediterranean diet are hard to ignore—they are less likely to develop high blood pressure, high cholesterol or become obese. Unhealthy lifestyle, diet and obesity have also been linked to type 2 diabetes, raised cholesterol and high blood pressure. These conditions can combine to make medical risks and problems more severe. Diet, lifestyle factors and obesity are also associated with an increased risk of certain cancers. Being substantially overweight can bring on or worsen osteoarthritis, sleep apnoea (a condition where your breathing stops for short spells during sleep), high blood pressure and gallbladder disease.

Traditional Mediterranean dishes consisting of large quantities of fresh fruits and vegetables, nuts, fish and olive oil—coupled with physical activity—reduce the risk of heart disease, certain cancers, diabetes, Parkinson's and Alzheimer's diseases. More specifically protecting against type 2 diabetes. Because Mediterranean dishes are rich in fiber, it slows down digestion and prevents huge swings in blood sugar. It also reduces the risk of having Parkinson's disease. In a diet containing high levels of antioxidants that prevent cells from undergoing a damaging process called oxidative stress, the risk of Parkinson's disease is practically cut in half.

Researchers investigated the lifestyle of the long-lived Mediterranean people to see if we could learn from them and use the knowledge in higher-risk populations. After such factors as smoking, exercise, education and stress had been taken into account; it was found that diet had played an essential part in keeping these communities healthy. The dietary pattern was not new. In fact, it was a traditional mix of fresh seasonal and easily stored produce that probably dated back to the early civilizations. It had incorporated new foods, such as tomatoes, peppers and potatoes. They tried to establish which foods offered particular health benefits, producing all the research into 'super foods'. It was found that both individual food components (such as vegetables, fruits, mono-unsaturated fats) and their combination into a long-term dietary pattern were important for health.

These cuisines are very ideal because it contain a variety of vegetables, a variety of fruit, legumes, cereals and cereal products; moderate quantities of fish, white meats, nuts, low-fat dairy produce; low quantities of red meat, eggs, sweets and sweet desserts; a high mono-unsaturated fat (eg, olive oil) to saturated animal fat (eg, fatty red meat); and low amounts of added salt - in many cases, herbs can be used for flavoring in place of excess salt. With fat being a major source of calories, restrictions can be placed on total amounts used in food preparation if setting targets for losing weight. There are many possibilities to be creative using locally sourced and affordable produce, according to your taste. You don't need to master Greek or Italian cookery - unless you want to. Just use the ingredient mix in any way you wish.

The health benefits of vegetables usually show in long run by improving your overall health and keeping the internal systems in perfect condition. The consumption of vegetables takes care of your digestive, excretory, and skeletal system, as well as blood pressure levels. With a diet rich in vegetables, you are being benefited with abundant antioxidants that keep away diseases like cancer, cardiovascular problems and strokes. Moreover, vegetables deliver ample amounts of vitamins, including folate, vitamin A, vitamin K and vitamin B6, as well as carotenoids like beta carotene from carrots, lycopene from tomatoes, zeaxanthin from greens, and lutein from spinach and collard greens. Vegetables also help in keeping your weight under control and promoting healthy skin and hair. There have been innumerable research studies done all over the world that strongly suggest having fresh, green vegetables on a regular basis is far better than going for supplementary tablets to get the wholesome nutrition that you need. Including vegetables in your diet is probably the easiest way to stay healthy, trim and nourished. Since vegetables are low-calorie, nutrient-rich foods, they help you to stay in optimum health over the long term by keeping your weight in check. According to a recent study, plant-based foods contain antioxidants (polyphenols) that may improve blood sugar in people at risk for diabetes and heart disease. We all know that Popeye made himself super strong by eating spinach, but you may be surprised to learn that he may also have been helping to protect himself against inflammatory problems, oxidative stress-related problems, cardiovascular problems, bone problems, and cancers at the same time. Calorie for calorie, leafy green vegetables like spinach with its delicate texture and jade green color provide more nutrients than any other food.

With the Mediterranean style, you'll eat mostly plant-based foods, including fruits and vegetables, potatoes, whole-grain bread, beans, nuts, and seeds. You can have yogurt, cheese, poultry, and eggs in small portions. You should eat fish and seafood at least twice a week. "Good" fats get a stamp of approval: think olives, extra-virgin olive oil, nuts, sunflower seeds, and avocados instead of butter or margarine. You'll use olive oil a lot while cooking. Reach for herbs and spices to add flavor. Doing it the Mediterranean way isn't focus on limiting total fat consumption, but rather on choosing healthier types of fat. The Mediterranean style of cooking features olive oil as the primary source of fat. Olive oil is mainly monounsaturated fat — a type of fat that can help reduce low-density lipoprotein (LDL) cholesterol levels when used in place of saturated or trans fats. "Extra-virgin" and "virgin" olive oils (the least processed forms) also contain the highest levels of protective plant compounds that provide antioxidant effects.

1. Braised Lamb Shanks

Ingredients:

6 lamb shanks (about 4 lb.)
1 tsp. herbes de provence
1/2 tsp. salt
1/2 tsp. pepper
1 tbsp. extra-virgin olive oil
1 tbsp. extra-virgin olive oil
2 onions (diced)
3 garlic cloves (minced)
1 bay leaf
1/2 tsp. dried oregano
1/4 tsp. salt
1/4 tsp. pepper
796 ml tomatoes
2 tbsps. granulated sugar
2 tbsps. balsamic vinegar
1 sprig fresh basil (or 1 teaspoon dried basil)
6 rosemary sprigs (for garnish)

Directions:

Using salt, pepper and herbes de provence, rub the lamb shanks with these spices and put it in a Dutch over medium-high heat. After heating the lamb shanks in batches, you can transfer it to a slow cooker.

To prepare the balsamic tomato sauce, use the fats drained from the oven. Use the oil along with onions, bay leaf, garlic, salt, oregano and pepper. Fry these ingredients for 5 minutes and stir. Cook and wait until the lamb is tender for about 6 hours.

Keep the lamb warm and covered. Set it aside. In a saucepan, pour cooking liquid until it gets thickened for about 15 minutes. Add some basil and you can now serve it with lamb. For garnishing, you may want to add rosemary sprigs.
To complete the dish, you can add mixed vegetables and mashed potatoes.

2. Crock Pot Mediterranean Pork With Couscous

Ingredients:

21/2 lbs. boneless pork loin (trimmed of fat, or the equivalent of boneless pork chops)
2 tbsps. olive oil
3/4 cup chicken broth
1/2 tbsp. paprika
1/2 tbsp. garlic powder
21/4 tsps. dried sage
1/4 tsp. dried rosemary
1/4 tsp. marjoram (dried)
1/4 tsp. dried thyme
1 tsp. oregano
1 tsp. basil
2 cups couscous (prepared according to package directions)

Directions:

Combine oil, broth and spices in a measuring cup. Cut the pork into small pieces (pork chops) and put it in a 4-quart slow cooker. Combine the mixture and put it all over the top of the pork. Cook the pork on low heat for about 7 to 8 hours until the meat is tender.

Shred the pork into pieces and put them back to the slow cooker. Add in the juices and serve.

3. Crock Pot Chicken Puttanesca

Ingredients:

3 lbs. boneless skinless chicken thighs

1 large onion, sliced thin

2 (6 ounce) cans tomato paste

1 (14 ounce) can diced tomatoes

1 green pepper (feel free to substitute with red)

8 ounces sliced baby bella mushrooms (you could add

more if you like)

6 chopped garlic cloves

3 teaspoons Italian seasoning

3 tablespoons capers

10 stuffed green olives (chopped) or 10 black olives

2 teaspoons kosher salt ((or more to taste)

1 1/2 teaspoons crushed red peppers

1/2 cup dry white wine (or cooking wine)

Directions:
Place the sliced onions at the bottom of the pot and place the chicken on top. Using a large bowl, add in all of the ingredients and the chicken. Cook everything on low heat for 7 hours.

4. Southern Italian Ratatouille

Ingredients:

(Serves 6)

3 1/2 tablespoons extra virgin olive oil

1/2 cup leek, white part only, thinly sliced

salt, to taste

fresh ground pepper, to taste

1 tablespoon garlic, minced

1 tablespoon fresh thyme, finely chopped

1/4 cup red bell pepper (1/4 inch dice)

2 green zucchini, diced (1/4 inch dice)

2 (400 g) cans chopped tomatoes

1 (150 g) packet Baby Spinach

100 g black olives, sliced

Directions:
When heated, put oil along with leek and garlic. Cook them for about 5 to 10 minutes.

Then, add the tomatoes, zucchini, red peppers and time and put it a slow cooker. Using low heat, cook the mixture for 5 hours.

Stir the mixture and put spinach one at a time. Combine the olives and leave it for about 20 minutes and the dish is ready to serve.

5. Mediterranean Lentil Soup with Spinach

Ingredients:

Servings: 6-8

Units: US

1 cup green lentils or 1 cup brown lentils

2 onions, chopped

2 celery ribs, finely chopped

2 carrots, finely chopped

1 potato, peeled and grated

1 clove garlic, minced

1 teaspoon cumin seed

1 teaspoon lemon, zest of

6 cups vegetable broth (chicken broth may be substituted)

1 (10 ounce) package frozen chopped spinach, thawed

2 tablespoons lemon juice

Directions:

1. Using cold water, sort and rinse the lentils.

2. In a crockpot, combine the lentils, celery, onions, potato, carrots, cumin seeds, garlic, vegetable broth and lemon zest.

3. Cook the mixture on low heat for about 8 to 10 hours or you may also use high heat for about 4 to 6 hours.

4. Combine the lemon juice and the spinach. Cook on high for 20 minutes.

6. Vegetarian Enchilada Casserole

Ingredients:

Servings:6

Units: US

1 (28 ounce) can crushed tomatoes

1 (14 ounce) jar chunky style prepared salsa

1 (6 ounce) can tomato paste

2 (16 ounce) cans black beans, rinsed and drained

1 lb. corn kernel, thawed if frozen

1 (4 ounce) can diced mild green chillies, drained

1 1/2 tablespoons ground cumin

1/2 teaspoon garlic powder

5 corn tortillas

2 ounces black olives, sliced and drained

Directions:
Put all of the 8 ingredients in a mixing bowl and mix them thoroughly.

Using your electric slow cooker, put about 1 cup of that mixture using low heat

Spread the mixture evenly and put 1 ½ tortillas on top.

Put the 1/3 of the mixture and spread in on the top.

Continue with the layering and end it with the last mixture.

Even out the top and sprinkle with olives.

Cook the dish for about 5 hours and serve it hot.

7. Mediterranean Pork Stew

Ingredients:

Servings:6

Units: US

2 lbs. boneless pork loin or 2 lbs. boneless pork shoulder,

cut into 1-inch pieces

1/3 cup flour

1/2 teaspoon ground cinnamon

1/2 teaspoon dried thyme

2 cups frozen pearl onions

1 (14 1/2 ounce) can chicken broth

3/4 cup dry red wine

1 tablespoon honey

1 tablespoon balsamic vinegar

hot cooked rigatoni pasta or rice

4 ounces crumbled feta or 4 ounces goat cheese

Directions:

In a 4 quart slow cooker, put the pork cubes with thyme, cinnamon, onions and flour.

In a separate bowl, mix the broth, honey, vinegar and wine.

Add the pork and cook it on low heat for 9 to 10 hours.

Wait until the pork is very tender.

Using soup plates, serve the dish alongside pasta or rice.

Garnish the dish with goat cheese.

8. Mediterranean Meatball Ratatouille

Ingredients:

Servings:6
Units: US
2 tablespoons olive oil, divided
1 lb. bulk mild Italian sausage
1 (8 ounce) package sliced mushrooms
1 small eggplant, diced
1 zucchini, diced
1/2 cup chopped onion
1 garlic clove, minced
1 teaspoon dried oregano leaves, divided
2 teaspoons salt, divided
1/2 teaspoon black pepper, divided
2 tomatoes, diced
1 tablespoon tomato paste
2 tablespoons chopped fresh basil
1 teaspoon fresh lemon juice

Directions:

Put 1 tbsp. of olive oil in a 5 quart slow cooker.

Cut the sausage into 1 inch meatballs and put half of them in a slow cooker.

Put half of the eggplant, mushrooms and zucchini and top them with garlic, ½ tsp. oregano, 1 tsp. salt, onion and ¼ tsp. pepper.

Use the remaining zucchini, meatballs, eggplant, mushrooms, ½ tsp. oregano, ¼ tsp. pepper and 1 tsp. salt.

Use 1 tbsp. olive oil to top the dish.

Cook the dish on low heat for 6 to 7 hours.

Stir the tomato paste and the diced tomatoes and cook on low for about 15 minutes.

Add in the basil and lemon.

Ready to serve

9. Mediterranean Style Beans And Vegetables Crock Pot

Ingredients:

Servings: 6

Units: US

1 (15 ounce) can great northern beans, drained and rinsed

1 (15 ounce) can red beans, drained and rinsed

5 teaspoons garlic, minced

1 large onion, chopped

1 cup carrot, thinly sliced

1/2 cup celery, thinly sliced

2 cups green beans, fresh, cleaned and cut

2 red chilli peppers, chopped (remove as many or as little

seeds depending on how much heat you want)

2 bay leaves

salt and pepper, to taste

Directions:

1. Put all of the ingredients in a crock pot and cook on low for 8 hours. Wait until the vegetables and beans are tender.

2. Take out the bay leaves and your dish is ready to serve.

10. Mediterranean Bean Soup

Ingredients:

Servings: 6

Units: US

1 lb. dried cannellini beans or 1 lb. dried navy beans

2 teaspoons salt

8 cups water

2 tablespoons olive oil

1 medium onion, chopped

1 bell pepper, chopped

2 carrots, chopped

1 celery rib, chopped

2 tablespoons garlic, minced (about 6 cloves)

1 bunch fresh kale

1 (14 ounce) can crushed tomatoes

1 teaspoon dried basil

1 teaspoon dried rosemary

1/4 teaspoon red pepper flakes

Directions:

1. Put the rinsed beans in a crock pot.

2. In high heat, add water and salt. Cook the dish for 8 hours.

3. In a skillet, heat the oil and add carrots, bell pepper, celery and onion.

4. Cook and stir for about 15 minutes.

5. Put the garlic and cook the dish for 3 to 4 minutes.

6. Include the vegetables and rinse the kale.

7. Chop the leaves and add it to the soup.

8. Add the tomatoes, rosemary, basil and red pepper flakes.

9. Cook until the kale is tender (15 to 20 minutes).

11. Crock Pot Mediterranean Stew

Ingredients:

Servings: 10

Units: US

1 butternut squash (peeled, seeded, cubed)

2 cups eggplants (cubed)

2 cups zucchini (cubed)

10 ounces frozen okra (thawed)

8 ounces tomato sauce

1 onion (chopped)

1 carrot (sliced)

1/2 cup vegetable broth

1/3 cup raisins

1 garlic clove (chopped)

1/2 teaspoon cumin

1/2 teaspoon turmeric

1/4 teaspoon crushed red pepper flakes

1/4 teaspoon cinnamon

1/4 teaspoon paprika

Directions:
Combine all of the ingredients in a crock pot and cook on low heat for about 7 to 9 hours.

12. 9 To 5 Mexican Crock Pot Chicken

Ingredients:

Servings: 5-6

Units: US

8 -10 chicken thighs (without skin, preferred)

1 (6 ounce) can tomato paste

1 (1 1/2 ounce) packet dry enchilada mix

1 cup water

1/2 cup shredded Monterey jack cheese or 1/2 cup cheddar cheese

black olives, to garnish (optional)

sour cream, to garnish (optional)

green onion, to garnish (optional)

Directions:
In a crock pot, put the chicken thighs.

Using a separate bowl, combine the tomato paste, water and enchilada sauce.

Put the mixture on top of the chicken and cook on low for about 8 hours.

Change to high heat and add in cheese. In case the sauce appears to be thick, you can add in hot water.

Serve the casserole dish and garnish with source cream, black olives and green onion.

If desired, you may also add some lettuce with rice or salsa. This dish can also be   great burritos.

13. Mediterranean Beef Stew (Crock Pot)

Ingredients:

Servings: 4

Units: US

2 medium zucchini, cut into bite size chunks

1 lbs. beef stew meat

2 (14 1/2 ounce) cans Italian-style diced tomatoes (do not drain)

1/2 teaspoon ground pepper

1 (2 inch) cinnamon sticks (or 1/2 teaspoon ground cinnamon)

Directions:

1. In a 3 ½ quart slow cooker, put zucchini at the bottom.

2. Combine the stew meat along with the other ingredients and cook them on high for about 5 hours.

3. Stir stew ½ hour before servicing the dish. Remove the cover and continue to cook the dish for 30 minutes.

4. Remove the cinnamon and serve.

14. Mediterranean Lentil Soup With Spinach

Ingredients:

Servings: 6-8

Units: US

1 cup green lentils or 1 cup brown lentils

2 onions, chopped

2 celery ribs, finely chopped

2 carrots, finely chopped

1 potato, peeled and grated

1 clove garlic, minced

1 teaspoon cumin seed

1 teaspoon lemon, zest of

6 cups vegetable broth (chicken broth may be substituted)

1 (10 ounce) package frozen chopped spinach, thawed

2 tablespoons lemon juice

Directions:

1. Using cold water, sort and rinse the lentils.

2. Put the onions, lentils, carrots, celery, garlic, potato, lemon zest, cumin seeds and vegetable broth in a crockpot.

3. Cover the pot and cook on low for 4 to 6 hours.

4. Then, add lemon juice and spinach. Cook again for about 20 minutes.

15. Crock Pot Pepperoni Pizza Dip

Ingredients:

Servings: 14

Units: US

1 (14 ounce) jar pizza sauce

1 (6 ounce) package pepperoni, sliced, chopped

8 medium green onions, chopped

1/2 cup red bell pepper, chopped

1 (2 1/4 ounce) can black olives, sliced and drained

1 cup mozzarella cheese, shredded

1 (8 ounce) package cream cheese, softened and cubed

Directions:

1. In a 1 ½ quart slow cooker, combine the pizza sauce, onions, olives, pepperoni and bell pepper. Cover and cook the dish on low heat for about 3 to 4 hours.

2. Add in the cream cheese and mozzarella until they melt.

16. Moussaka

Ingredients:

Servings: 4-6

Units: US

1 medium eggplant, thinly sliced

2 (6 ounce) jars marinated artichoke hearts

3 medium potatoes

1 tablespoon basil

2 cups shredded muenster cheese

Directions:
1. Using a shallow pan, put some cooking spray and put on the eggplant slices per single layer.

2. Drain the artichoke hearts and reserve the marinade.

3. Put some of the marinade on the eggplant and save the remaining marinade.

4. Then, bake the eggplant for 20 minutes.

5. Slice the potatoes and spread half of them at the bottom of the slow cooker.

6. Sprinkle 1/3 of the basil.

7. Continue doing the layers until you achieve a 3 layer dish
.
8. Sprinkle with the remaining marinade.

9. Cook on low for about 8 hours.

10. Put on some cheese and wait until the cheese melts for about 15 minutes.

11. To complete the dish, you can serve with bread and green salad.

17. Mediterranean Pot Roast

Ingredients:

Servings: 6-8

Units: US

3 -4 lbs. boneless beef roast

1 teaspoon salt

1 tablespoon Italian seasoning

1 garlic clove, minced

1/2 cup beef broth

1/3 cup sun-dried tomato, chopped

1/2 cup kalamata olive, pitted

1/2 cup frozen pearl onions

Directions:
1. Put the beef roast in the CrockPot.

2. Add all of the ingredients and put it over the roast.

3. Cook for about 5 to 6 hours. You may also combine the ingredients using a freezer bag and freeze it until it is already and set. Put the ingredients into the pot and cook for 6 to 8 hours.

18. Slow Cooked Lemon Chicken

Ingredients:

6 bone-in chicken breast halves (12 ounces each), skin removed

1 teaspoon dried oregano

1/2 teaspoon seasoned salt

1/4 teaspoon pepper

2 tablespoons butter

1/4 cup water

3 tablespoons lemon juice

2 garlic cloves, minced

1 teaspoon chicken bouillon granules

2 teaspoons minced fresh parsley

Hot cooked rice

Directions:
1. Put the chicken stock into the CrockPot.

2. Wash the chicken before you put it to the CrockPot then add lemon juice.

3. Use the spices and rub it all over the chicken.

4. Add some lemon skins to the chicken.

5. Cook the dish on high for about 4 to 6 hours.

19. Crock Pot Mediterranean Beef Roast And Vegetables

Ingredients:

Yield: 4 to 6

Units: US

3 1/2 lbs. beef chuck roast

8 red potatoes

1/2 lb. baby carrots

4 garlic cloves, peeled, whole

1 teaspoon salt

1 teaspoon dried rosemary, crushed

1/2 teaspoon fresh ground black pepper

1/4 cup water

1/4 cup dry red wine

2 tablespoons cornstarch, dissolved in

2 tablespoons water

chopped parsley

Directions:

1. Put the carrots, garlic and potatoes in a slow cooker. Rub the beef road with salt, pepper and rosemary.

2. Place it on top of the vegetables then add some wine and water.

3. Cover the dish and cook on low for 1o to 11 hours.

4. Remove the roast and carve the pot roast. Make thin slices.

5. For the gravy, combine 2 cups of cooking liquid and add cornstarch. Blend it and mix. Cook the mixture for 1 minute.

6. You may garnish the dish with beef and vegetables then add the gravy.

20. Mediterranean Vegetable Stew

Ingredients:

Servings: 6-7

Units: US

1 medium eggplant, chopped

2 zucchini, chopped

1 red bell peppers or 1 green bell pepper, seeded, diced

1/2 cup onion, chopped

3 large tomatoes, chopped or 1 (14 1/2 ounce) can diced tomatoes

1 tablespoon tomato paste

2 (14 ounce) cans garbanzo beans, drained and rinsed

1 (14 ounce) can water-packed artichoke hearts, drained and quartered

1 1/2 teaspoons dried oregano leaves

fresh ground black pepper

salt

crushed red pepper flakes, to taste

Directions:

1. Except for the noodles, put all of the ingredients in a slow cooker and stir.

2. Cook on low for about 7 to 9 hours. You may serve the dish with hot noodles.

21. Crock Pot Pork Mediterranean Style

Ingredients:

Servings: 6-8

Units: US

1 (3 lb.) boneless pork shoulder

For the marinade

1/4 cup olive oil

1/4 cup lemon juice

2 teaspoons dried oregano

2 teaspoons dried mint

2 teaspoons mustard

2 teaspoons pesto sauce

6 crushed garlic cloves

salt and pepper

Directions:

1. Combine and mix all of the ingredients and put the roast in a bowl.

2. Pour half of the marinade. Cover and leave it in a cool place for about 10 to 12 hours.

3. When ready for cooking, preheat a frying pan.

4. Scrape the marinade along with the marinade in the bowl.

5. Once the skillet is hot brown, roast the sides for about 10 minutes.

6. Put it in the Crockpot and cook on low heat for about 8 to 10 hours.

7. Add 2 tbsp. of cream.

8. In serving the dish on buns or pita, you have to cook the pork for about 1 to hours.

22. Crock Pot Mediterranean Eggplant Salad

Ingredients:

1 red onion, sliced

2 bell peppers, sliced

1 large eggplant, quartered and sliced

1 24 ounce can whole tomatoes (I used Trader Joe's plum tomatoes)

1 tablespoon smoked paprika

2 teaspoons cumin

1 teaspoon salt

fresh black pepper to taste

juice of one lemon

Directions:

Put all of the ingredients in a slow cooker and cook it for about 7 to 8 hours. You may also want to try the dish with bread or toasted pita.

23. Mediterranean Rice And Sausage

Ingredients:

Servings: 4

Units: US

1 1/2 cups uncooked rice

1/2 cup olive oil (I use a little less)

4 cups V8 vegetable juice

1 large onion, chopped

1/2 green bell pepper, cut into strips

1 clove garlic, crushed

3/4 lb. bulk Italian sausage

1/2 teaspoon salt, to taste

Directions:

1. Put olive oil in brown rice.

2. Place the V-8 juice in a crockpot.

3. Combine garlic, onion and pepper.

4. Add the brown rice to crockpot.

5. Add the sausage and put some salt.

6. Cook the dish on high heat for 2 hours then cook it again on low for about 5 hours.

24. Mediterranean Chicken

Ingredients:

Servings: 6-8

Units: US

4 -6 chicken breasts

2 cups diced frozen onions

1 teaspoon saffron

4 -6 cinnamon sticks

1 cup sliced almonds

1 1/2 teaspoons season salt

1 teaspoon red pepper flakes

Directions:
1. Except for the onions, combine all of the ingredients in a crockpot.

2. Cook it for about 6 to 8 hours on low heat.

3. Add half of the diced onions.

4. You may adjust the seasonings depending on your desired taste.

25. Sausage With Beans And Escarole

Ingredients:

12 ounces chicken sausage with Mediterranean seasonings, cut into 1/4-inch rounds

1 15-oz. cans cannellini beans, drained and rinsed

1 15-oz. cans garbanzo beans, drained and rinsed

1 28-oz. cans whole tomatoes, drained and chopped

1 1/2 cups canned low-sodium chicken broth

1 bay leaf

1 teaspoon dried thyme

1/4 teaspoon crushed red pepper

1 small head escarole, chopped

1/4 cup coarsely grated Parmesan

2 tablespoons chopped fresh parsley

Salt and pepper

Preparation:

1. Put the beans, tomatoes, sausage, broth, thyme, red pepper and bay leaf in a slow cooker. Cook for about 4 hours over low heat.

2. Stir the escarole and cook for 5 to 8 minutes more. Add in the parsley and Parmesan. Add pepper and salt. Season to taste and serve.

26. Shredded Mediterranean Chicken A La Crock Pot

Ingredients:

2 chicken breasts

1/2 onion

2 tablespoon(s) brown sugar

1/2 cup(s) capers

1 1/2 cup(s) kalamata olives

1 tablespoon(s) minced garlic

1 1/2 cup(s) chopped artichoke hearts

1/2 cup(s) chopped sundried tomatoes

1 cup(s) fresh chopped tomato

1/2 teaspoon(s) red pepper flakes

1/2 teaspoon(s) Italian seasoning

Preparation

1. Use half of your desired spaghetti sauce and toss your all of your fridge staples. (Use the measurements above for reference).

2. Put it in the pot and it will be ready to serve.

27. Mediterranean Pork In The Slow Cooker

Ingredients:
Serves: 2
approx. 330g diced pork
1 sweet potato, peeled and cut into chunks
1 courgette, cut into rounds
1 yellow pepper, sliced
drizzle of olive oil
2 large onions, thickly sliced
1 clove garlic, finely chopped
250ml pork stock
squirt tomato puree
good pinch dried oregano
freshly ground pepper
large handful whole button mushrooms (or thickly sliced field mushrooms)

Directions:
Prep: 5 minutes
Cook: 5 hours
Ready in:5 hours 5min
1. Combine sweet potato, pork yellow pepper and cour-gette. Put them into the slow cooker over low heat.

2. Fry the onions for a few minutes then add the garlic then stir again for a minute then transfer it to the slow cooker. Using the same fry pan, add the oregano, tomato puree and stock. Boil the mixture then transfer it to the slow cooker.

3. Add some pepper and cook for 4 hours over low heat. Then, add mush rooms. Cook again for one hour more then you can now serve the dish with bread or pasta.
Substitution

Instead of white potato, you may want to use sweet potato.

28. Mediterranean Roast Turkey

Ingredients:
2 cups chopped onion (about 1 large)
1/2 cup pitted kalamata olives
1/2 cup julienne-cut drained oil-packed sun-dried tomato halves
2 tablespoons fresh lemon juice
1 1/2 teaspoons minced garlic
1 teaspoon Greek seasoning mix (such as McCormick's)
1/2 teaspoon salt
1/4 teaspoon freshly ground black pepper
1 (4-pound) boneless turkey breast, trimmed
1/2 cup fat-free, lower-sodium chicken broth, divided
3 tablespoons all-purpose flour
Thyme sprigs (optional)

Preparation:
1. Combine all of the first 9 ingredients your slow cooker then add the ¼ cup of chicken broth.

2. Cover and cook for 7 hours over low heat.

3. In a small bowl, add the remaining ¼ cup broth and flour. Stir and whisk. Add the broth into the slow cooker. Cover and cook for 30 minutes. Slice the turkey and your dish is ready to serve.

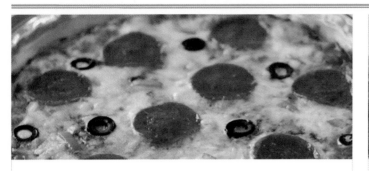 

29. Hot And Cheesy Pepperoni Pizza Dip

Ingredients:

1 15 ounce can of Good Pizza Sauce

3/4 cup Pepperoni Slices, chopped

4 Green Onions, Finely Chopped

1 Can Black Olives, Drained and Sliced

1/2 Roasted Red Pepper, Seeded and Diced

1/3 teaspoon Dried Oregano

1/8 teaspoon Garlic Powder

1/3 teaspoon Dried Basil

Salt and Pepper to Taste

1 1/4 cups Whole Milk Mozzarella, Shredded

3 ounces Whipped Cream Cheese

Directions:
1. Combine the pizza sauce, pepperoni, green onions, olives, basil, oregano, garlic powder and S & P. Cook over medium heat and add the cream cheese and mozzarella. Wait until the cheese melts.

2. Turn to low heat and keep the dish warm. Stir as frequent as needed to make the right consistency for the dip then you can just garnish with basil and add some breadsticks.

30. Mediterranean Chicken With Pepperoncini And Kalamatas

Ingredients:

Original recipe makes 4 servings

12 pepperoncini peppers, rinsed and drained

1 cup sliced pitted kalamata olives

8 cloves minced garlic

3 1/2 pounds chicken leg quarters

1 1/2 teaspoons paprika

1/4 teaspoon salt

1/4 teaspoon fresh ground pepper

1/2 teaspoon grated lemon zest

1/2 cup fresh-squeezed lemon juice

1 cup sour cream

1/2 teaspoon paprika

Directions:
PREP: 20 minutes
COOK: 6 hrs. 30 minutes
READY IN: 6 hrs. 50 minutes
1. Put the pepperoncini at the bottom of your slow cooker and put garlic and olive slices on top.

2. Make sure that the chicken is rinsed and dry before placing it on top of pepperoncini. Sprinkle the chicken with lemon zest, salt, pepper and 1 ½ tsps. paprika.

3. Cover the dish and cook it on low heat for about 6 ½ hours. Serve the chicken to a warm plate.

4. From low to high heat, skim fat from the cooking liquid and blend in some sour cream. Let is simmer for about 8 to 10 minutes. Add in paprika, pepper and stir.

31. Belly Burner Chilli

Ingredients:

Original recipe makes 8 servings

3 pounds ground spicy pork sausage

2 cups chopped onion

3 (15 ounce) cans tomato sauce

3/4 cup water

1/2 cup chopped black olives

1/2 cup chopped green olives

1/2 teaspoon ground black pepper

1 tablespoon soy sauce

2 teaspoons chilli powder

1 (15 ounce) can kidney beans

Directions:
PREP: 25 minutes
COOK: 8 hrs.
READY IN: 8 hrs. 25 minutes
1. Using a large skillet, cook the sausage until it turns brow then drain the sausage and crumble.

2. Put altogether the sausage, tomato sauce, water, onion, green olives, black olives, soy sauce, pepper, beans and chili powder in a slow cooker. Cook it for about 8 hours on low heat.

32. Mediterranean Succotash

Ingredients:

1 cup organic vegetable broth $

1 cup chopped zucchini

1 cup chopped red bell pepper $

1/2 cup pitted kalamata olives, halved $

2 garlic cloves, minced

2 (15-ounce) cans cannellini beans, rinsed and drained

1 (14.5-ounce) can diced tomatoes, undrained $

1/4 cup chopped fresh parsley

2 tablespoons balsamic vinegar $

2 tablespoons fresh lemon juice

1/4 teaspoon freshly ground black pepper $

1 (10-ounce) package couscous

2 ounces crumbled feta cheese (about 1/2 cup) $

Directions:

1. Combine the initial 7 ingredients in a 4 quart electric slow cooker. Stir the ingredients well, cover and cook for about 4 hours. Add in parsley as well as the other 3 ingredients on the list.

2. Follow the package directions and omit the salt and fat. Once the dish is ready, you may serve over couscous and add some cheese on top.

33. Slow Cooker Mediterranean Braised Chicken

Ingredients:
2 tablespoons olive oil
1 cut-up whole chicken (4 to 5 lb), skin removed
3/4 teaspoon salt
1/4 teaspoon freshly ground pepper
1/2 cup dry white wine or non-alcoholic white wine
6 thin slices lemon
5 cloves garlic, finely chopped
1 large red onion, cut into wedges
1 teaspoon herbes de Provence
1 cup Progresso™ chicken broth (from 32-oz carton)
1 can (14 oz) Progresso™ artichoke hearts, drained, quartered
30 pitted green olives or pimiento-stuffed manzanilla olives
1/4 cup chopped fresh Italian (flat-leaf) parsley

Directions
1. Using cooking spray, put some to your 5 to 6 quart slow cooker. Then in a 12 in skillet, use and heat 1 tbsp. of oil. Put some pepper and salt on the chicken.

2. Cook half of the chicken pieces for 4 to 6 minus and wait until it is brown. Put the chicken in a slow cooker. Continue with the process until the remaining chicken pieces are cooked.

3. Pour in some wine then simmer the dish over medium heat. Pour it into the slow cooker then you can add garlic, onion, lemon and herbes de Provence. After that, you may now put the broth on top.

4. Cover and cook on low for about 4 hours.

5. Stir the olives and the artichoke hearts in your slow cooker. Cook for 30 minutes more then sprinkle some parsley.

34. Slow-Cooker Mediterranean Pot Roast

Ingredients:
1 boneless beef chuck roast (3 lb.)
1 teaspoon salt
1 tablespoon Italian seasoning
1 large garlic clove, finely chopped
1/3 cup sun-dried tomatoes in oil, drained and chopped
1/2 cup sliced pitted Kalamata or ripe olives
1/2 cup Progresso™ beef flavored broth (from 32-oz carton)
1/2 cup frozen pearl onions (from 1-lb bag)

Directions
1. In a 12 inch skillet, use some cooking spray and cook the beef over medium-high heat for 5 minutes. Once it is brown, you can sprinkle it with Italian seasoning, garlic and salt then remove the beef from the skillet.

2. Put the beef into a 4 to 5 quart slow cooker then add some olives and tomatoes all over the roast. Add onions as well as the broth.

3. Cook the dish for about 5 to 6 hours on low heat.

4. Take the beef from the slow cooker and let it stand for around 15 minutes. Slice the beef and serve it with the onions and beef juice from the cooker.

35. Slow Cooker Cilantro Lime Chicken

Ingredients:

Original recipe makes 6 servings

1 (16 ounce) jar salsa

1 (1.25 ounce) package dry taco seasoning mix

1 lime, juiced

3 tablespoons chopped fresh cilantro

3 pounds skinless, boneless chicken breast halves

PREP 10 minutes

COOK 4 hrs.

READY IN 4 hrs. 10 minutes

Directions:

1. Combine and stir the lime juice, taco seasoning, cilantro and salsa in a slow cooker.

2. Put the chicken breasts and coat the chicken with the salsa mixture.

3. Cook the dish on high heat for 4 hours. Shred the chicken and the dish is ready to serve.

36. Sweet corn Fritters With Slow-Cooked Tomatoes

Ingredients:

6 large, ripe plum tomatoes, halved

pinch of sugar

avocado cream, (see bottom of page) to serve

For the fritters

450g sweet corn - use fresh, frozen (defrosted) or canned (drained)

175g plain flour

1 tsp. baking powder

2 eggs and 2 yolks, beaten

125ml milk

25g butter, melted

2 spring onions, finely chopped

½ red chilli, deseeded and finely diced

juice ½ lime

25g feta cheese, crumbled

1 tbsp. each chopped basil and parsley

olive oil, for frying

For the olive salad

200g large black olives, stoned and chopped

4 large handfuls rocket

drizzle olive oil

squeeze lime juice

Directions:

Heat the oven at 150C. Season with tomatoes and some sugar and roast it for 40minutes.

In using fresh corn, make sure that you remove the kernels then cook it in boiling water for about 4 to 5 minutes then drain. Separate the baking powder and the flour then add the milk, the yolks and the egg. Whisk the butter and the milk.

Add some feta, herbs, lime juice, chilli and spring onions unto the corn.

Use 2 to 3 tbsp. of the mixture in a frying pan and cook it for about 3 minutes. Transfer it to the oven and repeat the process until you finish the last one.

For your salad, combine rocket, herbs and olives then put some lime juice and oil. The salad goes with avocado cream, tomato halves and the fritters to complete the dish.

37. Greek Lamb With Spinach And Artichokes

Ingredients:

2 - 2 1/2 pounds boneless lamb shoulder roast

1 19 ounce can cannellini beans (white kidney beans),

rinsed and drained

1 14 1 /2 ounce can dice tomatoes, undrained

6   cloves garlic, minced

1/2 teaspoon salt

1/2 teaspoon dried oregano, crushed

1 14 ounce can artichoke hearts, drained and quartered

3   cups fresh baby spinach

3   cups hot cooked orzo pasta (Rosa marina)

 Crumbled feta cheese (optional)

Directions

1. Reduce the fat from the meat and cut it into pieces about 1 inch of size. Then, put the oregano, salt, garlic, tomatoes, beans and the mean in a 3 ½ or 4 quart slow cooker and stir.

2. Using low heat, cook it for about 8 to 10 hours. Add and stir spinach and artichoke hearts.

3. To complete the dish, you may add some lamb mixture and sprinkle cheese.

38. Slow Cooker Chicken Fajitas

Ingredients:

3 green, yellow or red peppers, sliced

2 onions, sliced $

2 tablespoons garlic, finely minced

8 boneless, skinless chicken breasts, cut into thin strips $

2-1 1/4-oz. packages taco seasoning mix

1 teaspoon coarse salt, divided $

1/2 cup olive oil $

8 to 12 flour tortillas $

Toppings: salsa, guacamole, sour cream, shredded Colby Jack cheese, chopped black olives, diced tomatoes, shredded lettuce

Preparation:

1. In a slow cooker, layer half of the chicken, garlic, onions and peppers then put 1 package of taco seasoning and ½ tsp. of salt. Continue layering and sprinkle oil.

2. Cook on low heat for about 4 to 6 hours. Make sure that there is no juice left. Stir and use the chicken mixture for your tortillas.

39. Garlic Lemon Chicken

Ingredients:

Serves 6

12 skinless chicken breasts and thighs (or other assorted pieces)

8 oz. black olives

2 lemons, divided

8 cloves garlic, peeled

2 springs rosemary

1 white onion, diced

1 cup low-sodium chicken broth

1/2 cup water

2 tablespoons olive oil

1 teaspoon dried oregano

kosher salt and freshly ground pepper, to taste

Directions:

Season chicken with oregano, pepper and salt. Heat 1 tbsp. of olive oil over medium-high heat. Add the chicken to the pan and cook it for about 3 minutes.

Put 1 tbsp. of olive oil and cook the remaining chicken. Set it aside.

Once done, transfer the chicken as well as the juices to the slow cooker. Put onion, olives, garlic, water, chicken broth, 1 lemon juice and rosemary.

Slice the remaining lemon and put the thin lemon slices all over the chicken.

Cover and cook the dish on low heat for about 5 to 6 hours. Optional: You may want to use a serving platter then pour the cooking liquids in a sauce pan over medium-high heat. Add 1 to 2 tbps of butter and 1 to 2 tbps of flour to create a gravy sauce.

40. Easy Traditional Greek Gyros

Ingredients:

Gyros

4 cloves garlic, minced or grated

1 onion, thinly sliced

1 - (2-3) pound boneless pork shoulder roast (or butt)

2 tablespoons dried oregano

2 teaspoons dried dill

2 teaspoons paprika

1/4 teaspoon cayenne pepper

1/4 - 1/2 teaspoon crushed red pepper

1 teaspoon salt

1 teaspoon pepper

2 lemons, juiced

1/3 cup olive oil

3 teaspoons red wine vinegar

3 tablespoons Greek yogurt

4-8 homemade or store bought pitas

1/2 cup fresh cherry tomatoes, halved, for serving

1 red onion, thinly sliced, for serving

4 ounces crumbled feta cheese, for serving

Tzatziki

1 cup plain Greek yogurt (I used full fat)

1/4 hothouse cucumber, peeled and seeded and diced small

1 large clove garlic, grated (or finely minced)

1/2 tablespoon white wine vinegar

1/2 teaspoon, dried dill

1 teaspoon dried oregano

1 tablespoon fresh lemon, juiced

1 tablespoon extra-virgin olive oil

Tapenade (optional)

1/4 cup pitted kalamata olives

1/4 cup pitted green olives

1 clove garlic, grated

1 pepperoncini, diced (optional)

Directions:

1. Put some cooking spray and add the garlic and the onions.

2. Add altogether in a small bowl the following: salt, pepper, crushed red pepper, cayenne, paprika, dill and oregano. Use half of the mixture for the pork. Sprinkle it all over the pork.

3. Put some olive oil in a large skillet and heat it over medium-high. Then, add the pork and sear it on all sides (2 minutes). Wait until it is golden brown.

4. Season the pork with the remaining drippings and seasonings then put it into the crockpot. Put 1/3 cup of olive oil, wine vinegar, lemon juice, ¾ cup of water and Greek yogurt. Cook on low heat for 8 hours. If the meat lacks moist, you may add some water.

5. In preparing tzatziki, you need to have thick consistency for the yogurt. Then, mix the salt, lemon juice, pepper, Greek yogurt, garlic, diced cucumber, white wine vinegar dill and oregano. Put some olive oil then refrigerate for about 30 minutes.

6. If you want to make the tapenade, make diced olives and mix it using a small bowl along with parsley, pepperoncini and garlic. Set it aside.

7. After waiting for 8 hours, take the pork and transfer it into the crockpot. Toss some onions and cook the dish to high heat. Allow the pork to warm for about 5 minutes.

8. You can heat the pitas then top the pitas with the following: tapenade, feta cheese, red onion, sliced tomatoes, tzatziki sauce and chicken.

41. Crock Pot Chicken Tacos With Mexican Rice

Ingredients:

2lbs chicken breasts (about 4 large, or 5 medium,) cut in half

1 packet taco seasoning (or a double batch of homemade taco seasoning)

16oz jar salsa

Corn taco shells

Taco toppings: chopped tomato, lettuce, green onions, cheese, black olives, etc.

For the Mexican Rice (can easily be halved):

1 teaspoon extra virgin olive oil

1/4 cup minced onion

salt & pepper

1 cup salsa

1 cup jasmine rice

2 cups vegetable broth

Directions:

1. In creating chicken tacos, layer the chicken breasts at the bottom of the crock pot and sprinkle some taco seasoning then put the salsa. Cook on low heat for about 4 to 5 hours until the chicken is tender. Then, mix some cooking liquid.

2. Set the oven at 425 degrees then add the shredded chicken into the taco shells and pour cheese on top. Bake it for about 2 to 3 minutes or until the cheese melts. You may top it with your preferred toppings.

3. In cooking the Mexican rice, heat the oil using medium heat. Put in the onion and season with pepper and salt. Sauté the dish for 5 minutes. Combine the salsa, vegetable broth and rice. On low heat, cover and let it simmer for about 20 to 25 minutes. Serve the dish along with the Chicken Tacos.

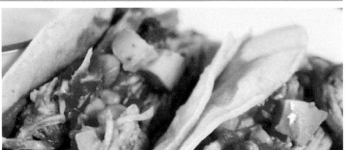

42. Crockpot Mediterranean Chicken Ragù With Orecchiette

Ingredients:

1 + 1/2 cups chicken broth

1 can (14 ounce) petite diced tomatoes

8 artichoke hearts, cut in half

1 roasted red pepper, diced

3 fennel stalks, diced

1 yellow onion, diced

2 tablespoons capers

5 cloves garlic, minced

2 teaspoons dried Italian seasoning

1/4 cup fresh parsley, chopped

1 teaspoon sea salt

1/4 teaspoon black pepper

1 + 1/2 pounds chicken breasts or cutlets, boneless, skinless

8-12 ounces Orecchiette pasta

parmesan cheese, for serving

Directions:

1. Put in the tomatoes, broth, artichokes, fennel, red pepper, capers, garlic and onion. Mix in the pepper, salt and Italian seasoning. Put the mixture in the chicken breasts and cook it on low heat for 6 to 8 hours. Take the chicken and shred it using two forks. Put it back and stir.

2. Cook the pasta and once it is al dente, add in the sauce and warm the dish. Cook it for about 10 minutes until the pasta absorbs the sauce them top with parmesan cheese.

43. Slow Cooker Salsa Chicken Tacos and Rice Bowls

Ingredients:
2 cups (16 ounces) salsa (I like Green Mountain Gringo or Newman's Own)
1 can (6 ounces) large black olives, sliced
1/4 cup diced red onion
2 cloves garlic, minced
1 - 2 tablespoons diced pickled jalapeno or 1 fresh, optional (omit if using a "hot" salsa)
1 teaspoon white wine vinegar
1 teaspoon chili powder
1/2 teaspoon ground cumin
1/2 teaspoon dried oregano, crushed between fingertips
1 cup finely shredded cheddar or monterey jack (or a mix), plus more for serving
1 cup corn, optional
1 pound boneless, skinless chicken breasts
coarse salt and fresh black pepper
For Serving:
1 cup dried rice, cooked
or
taco shells
or both!
sour cream, for serving
diced avocado, for serving
shredded lettuce, for serving

Directions:
1. In a 3 to 5 quart crock pot, combine ¼ cup of water, salsa, onions, olives, jalapeno vinegar, garlic, cumin, chilli powder, corn and oregano. Set it on high heat and mix.

2. Slice the chicken breasts in half and use salt and pepper to season the chicken.

3. Cook the chicken on high heat for about 3 to 4 hours. Then, remove the chicken breasts and shred it into small pieces. Use salt and pepper to add seasoning to the sauce.

4. Put the chicken back and add cheese. If it is watery, you can remove the lid and leave it there for 15 minutes.

5. Serve alongside rice then add some avocado, sour cream and extra cheese.

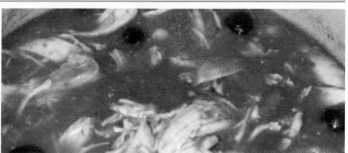

44. Slow Cooker Chicken Gyro Bowls

Ingredients:

2 lbs. boneless skinless chicken breast (or use skinless thighs)

2 cloves garlic, finely chopped or grated

1 teaspoon dried oregano leaves

1/2 teaspoon dried dill weed

Pinch of crushed red pepper flakes

1/2 teaspoon salt

1/2 teaspoon pepper

3 tablespoons olive oil

1 tablespoon red wine vinegar

Juice of 1/2 medium lemon

1/3 cup water

Tzatziki

16 oz. Yoplait® Greek 100 plain yogurt (from 2-lb container)

1/2 English (hothouse) cucumber or 1 regular cucumber, peeled, seeded and diced small

2 to 3 cloves garlic, grated or finely minced

1 tablespoon white wine vinegar

1 teaspoon dried dill weed

1 teaspoon dried oregano leaves

Salt and pepper, to taste

Juice of 1/2 medium lemon

1 tablespoon extra-virgin olive oil

Tortillas and Toppings

8 to 12 Old El Paso™ Stand 'N Stuff™ soft flour tortillas, heated as directed on package

1 red onion, sliced

1 cup grape tomatoes, sliced

1 cup crumbled feta cheese (4 oz.)

Directions:

1. Put some cooking spray in a 4 quart slow cooker then put all chicken ingredients into the slow cooker. Stir and cook on low for about 6 to 8 hours.

2. To make the Tzatziki, remove any liquid off from the surface of the yogurt and stir all of the Tzatziki ingredients in a bowl except for the oil. Drizzle 1 tbp of oil then cover it and put it on the fridge for about 30 minutes.

3. Take the chicken from the slow cooker and shred it into pieces and divide it among the tortillas. Top each tortilla with Tzatziki, grape tomatoes, feta cheese and red onion.

45. CrockPot Greek Chicken Soup with Garbanzos and Oregano

Ingredients:

3-4 cups diced, cooked chicken

1 can (15.5 oz.) garbanzo beans (chickpeas)

1 onion, diced small

1 can (14.5 oz) petite diced tomatoes with juice

2 T finely chopped fresh oregano (or use 2-3 tsp. dried oregano)

1 tsp. minced garlic (or use garlic puree from a jar)

1 tsp. Greek Seasoning (If you don't have Greek Seasoning, see note below.)

1 tsp. vegetable soup base (I like Better than Bouillon Organic Vegetable Base)

6-8 cups chicken stock, homemade or canned

1/2 cup chopped fresh parsley

crumbled Feta cheese for serving (optional, but very good)

Equipment: I used my favorite Crock Pot 3.5 Quart Slow Cooker, but any size that's close will work.

Directions:

Cut and make 3 to 4 cups of diced chicken. Use colander to rinse garbanzo beans then add the chopped onion and oregano along with all of the other ingredients into the crockpot except for the parsley. Cook it on low heat for about 8 to 10 hours.

Before serving the soup, chop the parsley. Then. Add the parsley to and cook for a few minutes. Serve the dish hot and put some crumbled Feta and additional parsley.

Note: For Greek seasoning, you can combine the following: oregano, garlic, salt, lemon peel, marjoram and black pepper.

46. Slow cooked lamb shoulder with blackcurrant glaze

Ingredients:
1.5kg lamb shoulder off the bone
For the marinade:
1tsp salt
1 tsp. pepper
1 tsp. cinnamon
1 tbsp. dried oregano
1 tsp. ground cumin seeds
3 large garlic cloves, finely chopped or grated
zest of 1 lemon
juice of 1/2 lemon
1/4 cup virgin olive oil
2 tbsp. virgin olive oil
3 medium brown onions cut into wedges
2 cups black current and apple juice
1 tbsp balsamic vinegar
2 tbsp raw honey

Directions:
1. Make large chunks of lamb shoulder then marinade it for a couple of hours.

2. Set the oven to 160 degrees Celsius then put the onion wedges as the bottom of the tray. Put 2 tbsp. of olive oil and drizzle some balsamic vinegar the put the lamb. Pour in the juice at the bottom and cover everything using an aluminum foil.

3 Cook the dish in the oven for about 3 ½ to 4 hours. Remove the tray and pour the juices into a sauce pan. Then, cook the lamb again for about 20 minutes while the oven is set at 200°C.

4. Add 2 tbsp. of honey, and blackcurrant juice. Simmer and cook the lamb for about 20 to 30 minutes.
5. Wait for 10 minutes before you serve the dish then put some caramelized onions on top.

6. For the salad dressing, cut a ripe pear into small cubes then add in 2 tbsp. of white wine vinegar or apple cider vinegar, ½ tsp of sea salt, 2 to 3 tbsp. of extra-virgin olive oil, ½ tsp. of Dijon mustard, ½ tsp of ground black pepper and ½ tsp. of ground coriander seed.

7. For the spiced yogurt, mix in pepper, paprika, ground cumin, a pinch of salt, chilli, a tbsp. of fresh paint and half cup of full fat yogurt.
Preparation time: 15 minutes plus marinating
Cooking time: 4-5 hours
Number of servings: 4-5

gravy sauce.

47. Slow Cooker Pepperoni and Chicken

Ingredients:

2 lbs. boneless, skinless chicken breasts

¼ tsp. salt

¼ tsp. black pepper

2¾ oz. turkey pepperoni (about 40 slices), sliced in half

¼ cup black olives, sliced

¾ cup reduced-sodium chicken broth

1 Tbsp. tomato paste

1 tsp. Italian seasoning

¾ cup shredded, low moisture, part-skim, shredded mozzarella cheese

Directions:
1. Put the chicken into a slow cooker then season with pepper and salt. Add the sliced pepperoni and olives into the cooker.

2. Using a bowl, whisk the tomato paste, Italian seasoning and chicken broth. Put the mixture into the cooker and cook it on low heat for about 6 to 7 hours.

3. Before you serve the dish, exactly 5 minutes before, put some cheese on top of the chicken and allow it to melt. .

4. Transfer chicken, olives and pepperoni with a slotted spoon.

48. Slow Cooker Mediterranean Roast Turkey Breast

Ingredients:

Original recipe makes 8 servings

1 (4 pound) boneless turkey breast, trimmed

1/2 cup chicken broth, divided

2 tablespoons fresh lemon juice

2 cups chopped onion

1/2 cup pitted kalamata olives

1/2 cup oil-packed sun dried tomatoes, thinly sliced

1 teaspoon Greek seasoning (such as McCormick's®)

1/2 teaspoon salt

1/4 teaspoon fresh ground black pepper

3 tablespoons all-purpose flour

Directions:

1. Put ¼ cup of chicken broth, turkey breast, onion, lemon juice, sun-dried tomatoes, kalamata olives, salt, paper and Greek seasoning into the slow cooker. Cover and cook on low heat for about 7 hours.

2. Using a bowl, put ¼ cup chicken flour and the flour and whisk until it is smooth. Add it into the cooker and stir. Cook it for about 30 minutes more.

49. Slow Cooker Mediterranean Hummus

Ingredients:

1-1/2 c. dried chick peas

water

1 tsp. sea salt

2 tsp. garlic, minced

1/4 c. olive oil

1/4 tsp. black pepper

1/4 c. lemon juice

1/2 c. cucumber, chopped

1/3 c. reserved juices from cooked chickpeas

Directions:

Rinse dried chickpeas. Put the beans in a crock pot and add water.

Cover and cook it on high heat for about 4 to 5 hours until the peas are soft.

If the pears are dry, you can add hot water.

Remove the chickpeas and put them into a food processor. Reserve and set aside the liquid left in the crock.

Then, put the cucumber, garlic, sea salt, lemon juice, olive oil and 1/3 cup cooking liquid left in the crock into the food processor. You may wish to add more cooking liquid until you get the right consistency.

After that, you can just put it in the fridge for hours then serve with veggies, chips or pita chips.

50. Slow Cooker Greek Rice Recipe with Red Bell Pepper, Feta, and Kalamata Olives

Ingredients:

1 T olive oil

1 3/4 cups Uncle Ben's Converted Rice

1 onion, chopped small

1 tsp. minced garlic

1 tsp. Greek Seasoning (I like Greek town "Billy goat" Seasoning from The Spice House.)

1 tsp. dried oregano (preferably Greek oregano)

2 cans (14 oz. each) chicken or vegetable stock (3 1/2 cups total)

1 red bell pepper, seeds removed and finely chopped

3/4 cup sliced Kalamata olives (or regular black olives will also be good)

3/4 cup crumbled Feta cheese

1/4 cup finely chopped fresh parsley

1 T fresh-squeezed lemon juice

Directions:
1. In a frying pan, heat the olive oil and sauté the rich until it is brown. Place the rice into the slow cooker.

2. Put the onions and cook it for 4 to 5 minutes. Add the dried oregano, Greek seasoning and the garlic and cook it for a few minutes more. Add the stock and remove any bits left then pour the stock mixture into the slow cooker along with the rice. Cook it on high heat for 1 ½ hours.

3. Chop the red bell peppers and after cooking the rice, add the red bell peppers and cook it for additional 15 minutes. Crumble the Feta and put the olives. Cook again for 15 minutes more.

4. Stir the chopped parsley and squeeze the lemon juice. Serve the dish hot.

51. Slow Cooker Spanish Roast

Ingredients:

1 tablespoon vegetable oil

1 (4 pound) beef chuck roast

salt and pepper to taste

1 cube vegetable bouillon

1 cup boiling water

1 (4 ounce) package sliced pepperoni

1 medium onion, quartered and thinly sliced

1 (15 ounce) can whole black olives, drained

2 tablespoons chopped fresh garlic

1 (14.5 ounce) can stewed tomatoes

Directions:
1. In a skillet, heat the oil over medium heat. Cook the roast on all sides then put some pepper and salt. Place it in the slow cooker.

2. Put the vegetable bouillon in boiling water then put into the cooker. Add the tomatoes, onion, pepperoni, garlic and black olives.

3. Cook it on high heat for about 4 hours.

52. Slow Cooker Mediterranean Beef Stew with Rosemary and Balsamic Vinegar (Low-Carb, Gluten-Free, Paleo)

Ingredients:
1-2 T olive oil (depends on your pan)
8 oz. sliced mushrooms
1 onion, diced in 1/2 inch pieces
2 lbs. trimmed and diced chuck steak, cut in bite-sized pieces (about 2-3 cups meat, for stove-top cooking I might use a more tender cut of beef)
1 cup beef stock (use 2 cups for stovetop cooking)
1 can (14.5 oz.) diced tomatoes with juice
1/2 cup tomato sauce
1/4 cup balsamic vinegar (I like Fini brand)
1 can black olives, cut in half or fourth
1/2 cup garlic cloves, cut in thin slices (optional, but good)
2 T finely chopped fresh rosemary (or use 1 T dried cracked rosemary)
2 T finely chopped fresh parsley (or use 1 T dried parsley)
1 T capers (or more)
fresh ground black pepper and salt to taste

Directions:
1. Heat some olive oil in a pan then add mushrooms. Sauté for minutes then put the mushrooms into slow cooker. Add a little bit more oil then sauté the diced onions for 5 minutes.

2. Put mushrooms to slow cooker then put some more oil along with the diced beef. Cook the beef for 10 to 15 minutes before putting it into the slow cooker.

3. Add 1 cup of beef stock and simmer it for a few minutes. Put the stock into the slow cooker and put some black pepper, capers, parsley, rosemary, garlic, olives, balsamic vinegar, tomato sauce, tomatoes and juice. Stir the mixture and cook on low heat for 6 to 8 hours. Season with salt and pepper.

53. Slow Cooker Mediterranean Stew

Ingredients:

Original recipe makes 10 servings

1 butternut squash - peeled, seeded, and cubed

2 cups cubed eggplant, with peel

2 cups cubed zucchini

1 (10 ounce) package frozen okra, thawed

1 (8 ounce) can tomato sauce

1 cup chopped onion

1 ripe tomato, chopped

1 carrot, sliced thin

1/2 cup vegetable broth

1/3 cup raisins

1 clove garlic, chopped

1/2 teaspoon ground cumin

1/2 teaspoon ground turmeric

1/4 teaspoon crushed red pepper

1/4 teaspoon ground cinnamon

1/4 teaspoon paprika

Directions:
1. Put altogether the eggplant, zucchini, tomato sauce, butternut, okra, tomato, carrot, onion, raisins, garlic and broth. Then season it with paprika, cumin, red pepper, turmeric and cinnamon.

2. Cook the dish on low heat for about 7 to 8 hours.

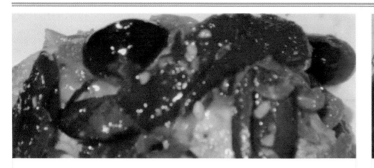

54. Slow Cooker Mediterranean Pork Roast

Ingredients:

2   fennel bulbs, trimmed and sliced

1   boneless pork loin roast (about 3 pounds), trimmed

4   teaspoons Greek seasoning mix (such as McCormick)

4   plum tomatoes, chopped

1/3 cup plus 2 tablespoons low-sodium chicken broth

3/4 teaspoon salt

1/2 teaspoon black pepper

2 cornstarch

1 1/2 teaspoons Worcestershire sauce

1/4 cup chopped black olives (optional)

Directions:
Put a fennel in the slow cooker bowl. Season your pork using 1 tsp. of Greek seasoning then place it on top of the fennel.

2. Cover the pork with tomatoes and put 1/3 cup of the broth into the slow cooker   bowl. On top of it, put 2 tsps. of Greek seasoning, ¼ tsp. of pepper and ½ tsp. of salt. Cook the dish on high heat for about 3 hours or on low heat for 6 hours.

3. Stir and blend the 2 tbsp. broth, Worcestershire and cornstarch. Put the pork to a serving platter. Remove the liquid from the slow cooker and put in a sauce pan. Mix in the vegetables around the pork.

4. Over medium-high heat, boil the liquid then combine the cornstarch mixture. Whisk it and add 1 tsp. of Greek seasoning, ¼ tsp. pepper and ¼ tsp. salt. Cook for about 1 minute and pour the sauce all over the pork. You may also top it with olives.

55. Slow Cooked Mediterranean Chicken

Ingredients:

1 chicken, about 4 lb., cut into 8 pieces

Salt and freshly ground pepper, to taste

2 Tbs. olive oil

1 jar Mediterranean chicken braising base

Directions:
Use salt and pepper to season the chicken.
Slow-cooker method: Using a fry pan, heat the olive oil over medium-high heat and cook the chicken for about 8 to 10 minutes. Put the chicken into a slow cooker then combine the braising base. Cover the top and cook on high heat based on the instructions provided or wait until the meat is tender (3 hours).

Oven method: Set the temperature at 325°F, heat the olive oil and the chicken in your oven. Put the chicken to the pot then out the braising base. Simmer and cover the pot before transferring it back to the oven. Then, cook for about 2 to 2 ½ hours.

Once cooked, put the sauce and chicken to a serving bowl and your dish is ready to serve.

56. Mediterranean Chicken Casserole

Ingredients:

2 teaspoons olive oil

8 chicken lovely legs

1 large brown onion, halved, thinly sliced

3 celery sticks, trimmed, cut into 2cm-thick slices

2 garlic cloves, crushed

200g button mushrooms, thickly sliced

2 x 400g cans diced Italian tomatoes

1 chicken stock cube (Massel brand)

150g (1 cup) frozen broad beans, thawed, peeled

1 tablespoon fresh thyme leaves

Freshly ground black pepper

200g dried spiral pasta, optional, to serve

Directions:

1. Set the oven temperature at 180°C then heat the oil over medium heat. Put the chicken and cook it for about 5 minutes. Transfer the chicken to an 8 cup casserole dish.

2. Combine the celery and the onion to the frying pan. Stir and cook for about 5 minutes. Add the mushroom and garlic. Stir and cook again for another 2 minutes. Put the stock cube and tomato. Stir and cook for 2 minutes. Once done, add this to the casserole dish.

3. Cover the casserole dish using a foil and bake it for about 35 minutes. Put half of the thyme and the broad beans then cook aging for 10 minutes. Take the dish out of the oven and season it with pepper.

4. In cooking the pasta, follow the instructions in the packet or cook until it is al dente.

5. Put the casserole in a large bowl along with the pasta then sprinkle with thyme.

57. Slow Cooker Mediterranean Beef and Pasta

Ingredients:

1 lb. beef stew meat

½ cup chopped onion

1 can (14 oz.) artichoke hearts, drained, chopped

1 jar (4.5 oz.) Green Giant™ sliced mushrooms, drained

1 can (14.5 oz.) diced tomatoes, undrained

1 tablespoon balsamic vinegar

1 tablespoon drained capers

1 tablespoon dried minced garlic

1 teaspoon Italian seasoning

1 teaspoon salt

1 teaspoon sugar

1 ½ cups uncooked penne pasta

1 tablespoon olive oil

Fresh ground pepper, if desired

½ cup shredded Parmesan cheese

Directions:

1. Using cooking spray, put some in a 3 ½ to 4 quart slow cooker then combine all of the ingredients excluding the cheese, pepper, oil and pasta.

2. Cover the top and cook on low for about 7 to 9 hours.

3. 15 minutes before serving the dish, cook the pasta based on the direction. Stir the pasta, add oil and pepper into the mixture then put some cheese.

58. Mediterranean Roast Turkey

Ingredients:

2 cups chopped onion (about 1 large)

1/2 cup pitted kalamata olives

1/2 cup julienne-cut drained oil-packed sun-dried tomato halves

2 tablespoons fresh lemon juice

1 1/2 teaspoons minced garlic

1 teaspoon Greek seasoning mix (such as McCormick's)

1/2 teaspoon salt

1/4 teaspoon freshly ground black pepper

1 (4-pound) boneless turkey breast, trimmed

1/2 cup fat-free, lower-sodium chicken broth, divided

3 tablespoons all-purpose flour

Thyme sprigs (optional)

Directions:

1. In an electric slow cooker, put altogether the first 9 ingredients in the recipe. Then, include the ¼ cup of chicken broth. Cover the top and cook on low heat for 7 hours.

2. Put the remaining ¼ flour and broth in a bowl. Stir and whisk until it is smooth before adding the broth mixture into the slow cooker. Cook on low heat for half an hour. Then add the sliced turkey.

59. Mediterranean Chicken with Tomatoes, Olives and Capers Recipe

Ingredients:

1 1/2 pounds boneless, skinless chicken thighs

salt and pepper

1 tablespoon olive oil

1 medium onion, chopped

3 cloves garlic, chopped

1 teaspoon dried thyme

1 teaspoon dried rosemary

1/4 cup red wine

1/4 cup kalamata olives, pitted

2 tablespoons capers, rinsed and drained

1 1/2 cups chopped tomatoes

fresh lemon zest

Directions:

1. Using salt and pepper, season the thigh. Heat olive oil in a 5 quart pressure cooker then put in the rosemary, thyme, onions and garlic. Sauté for about 3 to 4 minutes.

2. Put the chicken pieces and cook both sides. Pour red wine and cook for 2 to 3 minutes. Add the tomatoes, capers and olives. Turn to high pressure then cook it for 15 minutes. Once the dish is ready, you may want to sprinkle it with some lemon zest.

60. Slow-Cooker Mediterranean Minestrone Casserole

Ingredients:

3 medium carrots, sliced (1 1/2 cups)

1 medium onion, chopped (1/2 cup)

1 cup water

2 teaspoons sugar

1 teaspoon Italian seasoning

½ teaspoon salt

¼ teaspoon pepper

1 can (28 ounces) diced tomatoes, undrained

1 can (15 oz.) Progresso™ garbanzo beans, rinsed and drained

1 can (6 ounces) Italian-style tomato paste

2 cloves garlic, finely chopped

1 ½ cups Green Giant™ Steamers™ frozen cut green beans (from 12 oz. bag), thawed

1 cup uncooked elbow macaroni (3 1/2 ounces)

½ cup shredded Parmesan cheese (2 ounces)

Directions:

1. Combine all of the ingredients except the cheese, macaroni and green beans in a 3 to 4 quart slow cooker.

2. Cover the top and cook it on low heat for about 6 to 8 hours.

3. Add the green beans and macaroni then stir. Turn to high heat setting and cook for about 20 minutes. Wait until macaroni and the beans are tender. Put some cheese on top.

Expert Tips

Instead of using garbanzo beans, you can use a can of northern beans. For cooked beans, you can just use 1 ¾ cups instead of the can. For a more balanced flavor, you may want to add just right amount of sugar.

61. Slow Cooker Mediterranean Salmon

Ingredients:

1 pound salmon fillets

1 teaspoon garlic powder, divided

1 teaspoon onion powder, divided

1 tablespoon Italian seasoning, divided

½ teaspoon black pepper, divided

1 tablespoon olive oil, divided

3 garlic cloves, sliced

½ onion, sliced

1 zucchini, quartered and sliced

1 red bell pepper, julienned

1 tomato, chopped

Directions:

Spray in a 6 quart slow cooker with cooking spray.
Put the salmon fillets at the bottom of the oven dish. For the seasoning, use olive oil, black pepper, Italian seasoning, half of the garlic powder and onion powder.

Add the tomato, bell pepper, zucchini, onion and garlic then season with the remaining herbs, spices and olive oil. Toss the vegetables with the mixture.

Cover the dish and place it in the slow cooker. Cook on low for about 6 hours.

Serve the dish with whole grain pasta or you may also have it with couscous.

62. Mediterranean Style Slow Cooked Chickpeas

Ingredients:

300g dried chickpeas

1 tablespoon olive oil

2 brown onions, halved, coarsely chopped

3 garlic cloves, crushed

1 x 800g can diced Italian tomatoes

1L (4 cups) Campbell's Real Stock Vegetable

1 1/2 tablespoons fresh thyme leaves

2 tablespoons coarsely chopped fresh oregano

500g butternut pumpkin, deseeded, peeled, cut into 3cm pieces

4 zucchini cut into 3cm pieces

1 (about 400g) eggplant, cut into 3cm pieces

1/3 cup coarsely chopped fresh continental parsley

2 tablespoons fresh lemon juice

Crusty bread, to serve

Directions:

1. Put the chickpeas in a huge bowl and pour cold water. Soak it overnight then drain.

2. Using a sauce pan, heat the oil and add garlic and onion. Stir and cook for about 8 to 10 minutes. Wait until the onion softens. Add in the oregano, thyme, stock, tomato and the chickpeas. Turn to medium low heat and simmer. Cover and cook for about 1 ¼ hours.

3. Add the eggplant, zucchini and pumpkin. Cover and cook for 25 minutes. Stir the dish occasionally for about 15 minutes. Wait until the vegetables and the chickpeas are tender. Add the lemon juice and half of the parsley. Stir and combine. Season the dish with pepper.

4. Once ready, you may serve it with crusty bread.

63. Slow Cooked Mediterranean Bulgur and Lentils

Ingredients:

1 cup uncooked bulgur wheat or cracked wheat

½ cup dried lentils, sorted, rinsed

1 teaspoon ground cumin

¼ teaspoon salt

3 cloves garlic, finely chopped

1 can (15.25 oz.) whole kernel corn, drained

2 cans (14 oz. each) vegetable or chicken broth

2 medium tomatoes, chopped (1 1/2 cups)

½ cup drained pitted kalamata olives

1 cup crumbled reduced-fat feta cheese (4 oz)

Directions:

1. Combine all of the ingredients excluding cheese, olives and tomatoes in a 3 to 4 quart slow cooker.

2. Cover the top and cook it on low heat for 3 to hours.

3. Add in the olives and tomatoes then stir. Change the setting to high heat and cover. Cook for 15 minutes more. Sprinkle with some cheese on top.

Expert Tips

You can have almost everything in this recipe: cheese, vegetables and grains. You may want to add some pita bread wedges along with a green salad.

64. Slow Cooked Mediterranean Beef over Whole Wheat Orzo

Ingredients:

2 lbs. stew meat

1 large white onion, sliced

2 15 oz. cans tomato sauce

¼ cup sweet vermouth

½ cinnamon stick

1 large bay leaf

1 tsp. Greek oregano

Pinch of salt and pepper

Feta cheese, crumbled, for garnishing

1 lb. DeLallo whole wheat

Directions:

At the bottom of the slow cooker, put the sliced onion then add the meat and the rest of the ingredients.

Cover it and cook on low heat setting for about 8 hours. Meanwhile, boil the water then add the orzo. Drain and put some olive oil.

While serving, you can add the orzo and the right amount of meat sauce. Garnish with feta cheese and your dish is ready.

65. Mediterranean Seafood Stew

Ingredients:

2 large leeks, white and pale green parts only

1 1/2 pound(s) (2 large) fennel, trimmed and finely chopped

2 1/4 pound(s) tomatoes, chopped

2 clove(s) garlic, chopped

Salt

Pepper

4 sprig(s) fresh thyme

8 sprig(s) fresh flat-leaf parsley, stems and leaves separated

1 pound(s) mussels, beards removed, scrubbed

1 pound(s) shelled deveined 16- to 20-count shrimp

12 ounce(s) skinless cod fillet, cut into 4-inch pieces

2 teaspoon(s) extra-virgin olive oil

4 crusty dinner rolls

Directions:

Cut the leek into ¼ in slices (lengthwise) then remove the root ends. Put them in a huge bowl with cold water. Remove the grit and repeat the process then drain.

Put the leeks into a 6 quart slow cooker as well as ½ tsp. of ground black pepper, 1 tsp. salt, tomatoes, fennel and garlic. Using a kitchen twine, tie the parsley stems and thyme then put in the vegetable mixture.

Cover and cook on high heat setting for 3 hours. Add the mussels and the shrimp then stir. Put the fish on stop. Cover and cook for 30 to 40 minutes.

Put the mussels in the serving dishes then put 3 cups of stew to a container. Put it in the fridge overnight. Then, divide the stew among the dishes. Put some oil over the stew and sprinkle parsley over it. Serve your dish with rolls.

66. Slow Cooker Beef Vegetable Soup

Ingredients:

For the Slow Cooker Beef:

2 lb. oven roast

1 14.5 oz. can diced tomatoes with herbs and juice

2 tbsp. brown sugar

1 cup red wine

salt and pepper

For the soup:

Slow cooked oven roast beef, shredded

32 oz. chicken broth, plus 2 extra cups if needed

1 lb. frozen mixed soup vegetables

2 potatoes, peeled and small diced

1 bay lead

Directions:

1. Combine red wine, brown sugar, tomatoes and roast in the slow cooker.

2. Put generous amount of pepper and salt. Cover the lid and cook on low heat setting for 8 hours.

3. Take the roast and put it on a cutting board. Remove the fats and shred it using a form.

4. Put the meat into the slow cooker then add the bay leaf, veggies, potatoes and chicken stock.

5. Cover the lid and cook again for 4 hours on low heat.

67. Slow Cooker Mediterranean Chicken Stew

Ingredients:

2 teaspoons olive or vegetable oil

2 pounds boneless, skinless chicken thighs

1 teaspoon garlic salt

¼ teaspoon pepper

2 teaspoons dried oregano leaves

2 cans (14.5 ounces each) diced tomatoes with garlic and onion, undrained

1 can (14 ounces) quartered artichoke hearts, drained

1 package (10 ounces) couscous (1 1/2 cups)

1 can (6 ounces) pitted medium ripe olives, drained

Directions

In a 12 in. skillet, heat oil. Season chicken with oregano, garlic, salt and pepper then cook it in oil for about 8 minutes. Wait until chicken is brown then drain. Put the chicken as well as the artichokes and tomatoes in 4 to 4 ½ quart slow cooker.

Cover the lid and cook on low for about 5 to 6 hours. In cooking the couscous, follow the directions in the package. Add and stir the olives.

Once the dish is ready, put the stew over the couscous. Expert Tips

If you don't like onions, you can substitute diced tomatoes with roasted garlic with diced tomatoes with garlic and onion. You may also serve the dish with a spinach salad with feta cheese on top and some fresh figs. The dish also goes perfectly well with sesame bread.

68. Hearty Tuscan Slow Cooker Soup:

Ingredients:

13 oz. lite smoked sausage, sliced

1 large white potato peeled and small diced

8 oz. sliced button mushrooms

1 lb. frozen spinach

1 28 oz. can diced tomatoes and juice

1 48 oz. can chicken broth

1 15.5 oz. can great northern beans, drained and rinced

2 cloves garlic, minced

1/2 cup julienned carrots

salt and pepper to taste

shredded Parmesan cheese to garnish

Directions
1. Drizzle some olive oil in a cast iron skillet then cook the potatoes, mushrooms and sausage. Add them into the slow cooker.

2. Put the ingredients into the slow cooker then cook on low heat setting for about 8 hours.

3. Top the dish with Parmesan cheese.

69. Mediterranean beef brisket

Ingredients:

1 2- to 2-1/2 lb. beef brisket

1 tsp. kosher salt

1 tsp. fresh black pepper

2 tsp. olive oil

2 medium onions, chopped

2 large cloves garlic, peeled and sliced

1 Tbsp. Herbes de Provence (or 1 Tbsp. dried thyme leaf)

1 15-oz can diced tomatoes, drained (discard liquid)

2 tsp. Dijon mustard

1/2 cup dry red wine (for slow cooker or stovetop, use entire bottle of wine)

Directions
Trim the meat and add salt and pepper for seasoning. Using a nonstick frying pan, heat oil and cook the meat.

Put the meat to a 4 quart slow cooker and add the other ingredients. Pour a bottle of wine all over the meat then cook on low heat for 8 hours.

Transfer the meat to a serving platter. Extract some of the onion and tomato from the pot and put the vegetable mixture on top of the meat. Wait for 10 minutes before serving the dish.

70. Shrimp with Tomatoes and Feta from The Mediterranean

Ingredients:

¼ cup olive oil

1 medium onion, chopped

1 28-ounce can crushed tomatoes

½ cup dry white wine

½ teaspoon dried oregano

Salt

Pinch of crushed red pepper

1 ½ pounds medium shrimp, shelled and deveined

1 cup crumbled feta cheese [about 4 ounces]

2 tablespoons chopped fresh flat-leaved parsley

1 12-ounce Collins or sling glass

Directions:
Heat oil in a small skillet. Put the onion and cook for about 10 minutes. Using a large slow cooker, scrape the onion.

Add in the crushed pepper, salt, oregano, wine and tomatoes then stir. Cover the lid and cook on high heat for about 2 hours.

Rinse the shrimp with water before putting and stirring it with the sauce. Add some cheese and cook it on high heat for 10 to 15 minutes.

Serve the dish with some chopped parsley on top.

71. Mediterranean Slow Cooker Chicken and Potatoes

Ingredients:

4 small (2 pounds) bone-in chicken breasts

2 teaspoons Herbes de Provence

1 teaspoon garlic salt

Freshly ground pepper to taste

½ cup flour

1 tablespoon extra-virgin olive oil

1 ¼ pounds small red potatoes

¾ cup frozen, thawed pearl onions

1 cup small baby carrots

¾ cup chicken broth

8 ounces small baby bella or white mushrooms

Chopped fresh thyme (optional)

Directions::
Take the skin from the chicken breasts and set it aside. In a separate plate, mix pepper, salt, garlic and herbes de Provence. In another plate, put the flour and coat the chicken breasts.
Using a large skillet, heat the oil and cook the chicken over medium high heat.

Transfer the chicken into a bigger slow cooker then add in the remaining ingredients except for the thyme. Cover the lid and cook on high heat for 4 hours.

Sprinkle the dish with fresh thyme.

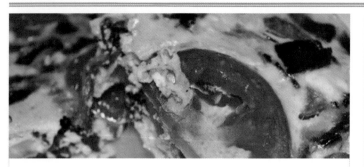

72. Slow-Cooker Crustless Mediterranean Quiche

Ingredients:

8 eggs

1 cup milk

1 cup Original Bisquick™ mix

2 cups chopped fresh spinach

1 1/2 cups crumbled feta cheese (6 oz.)

1/2 cup chopped roasted red bell peppers and/or sun-dried tomatoes

1/4 cup chopped fresh basil leaves

1 teaspoon finely chopped garlic

1 package (9.6 oz.) fully cooked sausage crumbles

1/4 cup crumbled feta cheese for garnish, if desired

Directions
In a 4 to 5 quart slow cooker, put some cooking spray. Combine and mix milk, egg and Bisquick mix in a slow cooker. Then, add in the sausage, garlic, basic, bell peppers and 1 ½ cups feta cheese and stir.

Cover the cooker and cook on high heat for 3 to 4 hours. When the edges are golden brown and the center is already set, quiche is needed.

Cut the pieces then put some feta cheese for garnishing.
Expert Tips

To have a perfect brunch menu, you can serve this dish alongside fresh orange slices, croissants and white grape juice.

If you do not have feta cheese, you can use mozzarella cheese or ½ cups of shredded pepper Jack.

73. Slow Cooker Three Pepper Tortellini Soup

Ingredients:

1 red bell pepper, diced

1 yellow bell pepper, diced

1 green bell pepper, diced

1/2 onion, diced

1 zucchini, halved and sliced

1 cup frozen corn

8 cups stock (chicken, beef, or veggie)

1 14.5 oz. can tomato sauce

1 14.5 oz. can diced tomatoes

1 lb. 90% lean ground sirloin

1 lb. frozen cheese tortellini

2 cups freshly grated cheddar cheese

small bunch chives, chopped

Directions:
Season the ground meat with salt and pepper and cook it in a skillet.

Put the diced veggies in the slow cooker then put in the corn, stock, diced tomatoes and tomato sauce.

When the meat is cooked, drain and add it to the slow cooker. Cover the lid and cook on low heat for 8 hours. Boil water and put in tortellini in a pot. When the tortellini rises on top, use a slotted spoon and place the tortellini into the slow cooker.

Stir and mix all of the ingredients.
Serve the dish with chives and cheese on top.

74. Slow Cooked Tuna Mediterranean Style: Tuna Confit with Black Olive Tapenade and Tomato Salsa

Ingredients:
4 half-inch. tuna steaks
1 preserved lemon sliced
6 tablespoons of chopped sun dried tomatoes
1 small onion halved and sliced thin.
1 celery stalk chopped
1 tablespoon of flat leaf parsley chopped
For the marinade:
1 tablespoon of preserved lemon juice
3 garlic cloves minced
1 teaspoon of dried thyme
1 teaspoon of dried rosemary
11/2 teaspoons of fleur de sel or other sea salt
1/2 teaspoon of red pepper flakes
zest and juice of one fresh lemon
1 cup of Extra Virgin Olive Oil (EVOO)

Directions:
Put all of the marinade ingredients in a huge bowl. Whisk marinade ingredients together in a large bowl.

Add the parsley, celery, onion, sun dried tomatoes and lemon slices into the marinade.

Put 1/3 of the marinade in a freezer bag and put 2 tuna steaks on the marinade. Put 1/3 of the marinade over the steaks. Pout the remaining marinade on the steaks. Place them inside the fridge for 4 hours.

Set the oven temperature at 250 degrees.

Put the tuna steaks and the marinade in a baking pan. Lay the tomatoes, celery, onion and lemon all over the steaks. Use a parchment and put it in the fan then seal the pan using an aluminum foil

Bake the dish for 40 minutes.

Serve with salsa or tomato salad. The dish also goes well with mashed potatoes or rice.

75. Slow Cooker Mediterranean Chicken With Polenta

Ingredients:
1 1/2 pounds chicken breast, boneless and skinless

4 ounces cheese, feta, crumbled

2 cups spinach, fresh baby, chopped

1/4 cup pesto sauce (prepared)

1/4 cup sundried tomatoes, chopped

1 can (15 ounces each) tomatoes, canned with Italian seasoning

6 ounces mushrooms, Crimini or button or combo, sliced

1/4 teaspoon garlic powder

1/4 teaspoon salt

1/4 teaspoon pepper, black, ground

6 ounces polenta, precooked

Directions:
1. In a small bowl, chop the spinach and the sundried tomatoes. Put in the pesto and feta cheese.

2. Cut the chicken breast at the center. Do not cu all the way through. Open it the chicken breast and add spinach mixture. Close and secure using toothpicks.

3. Put the chicken into the slow cooker and lay the mushrooms and the tomatoes on top of the chicken. Use garlic powder, pepper and salt for seasoning. Put the sliced polenta (1/2 inch thick) on top of the tomatoes.

4. Cover and cook on high heat setting for 3 ½ or 4 hours. Divide the chicken and the polenta in 4 plates then top with mushrooms and tomatoes.

76. Spiced Meatballs and Slow-Cooked Eggplant, Zucchini and Peppers

Ingredients:
Slow-Cooked Eggplant, Zucchini and Peppers
1 small eggplant, chopped
1 large zucchini, chopped
1 red or green bell pepper, seeded and chopped
1 yellow onion, chopped
12 cherry tomatoes cut in half
Juice from 1/2 lemon
1 tbsp. olive oil
salt and pepper to taste
handful of herbs (such as basil, coriander or parsley), chopped
Spiced Meatballs
1/2 lb. ground beef
1 tsp. ras al hanut
1/2 tsp. cumin
1/2 tsp. salt
1/2 yellow onion, finely chopped
1 tsp. olive oil

Directions
1. Heat oil and add onion. Cook until it is golden brown. Then, add pepper and sauté.

2. Put the eggplant and sauté for a few minutes.
3. Add zucchini and turn the heat setting to low. Stir and cook for 20 to 30 minutes.

4. Add salt, pepper and tomatoes then cook for 5 minutes more.

5. Add the herbs and lemon juice then put seasoning depending on preference.

Spiced Meatballs
For the spiced meatballs, mix the meat and form them into meatballs.
Mix together and form into meatballs.
Heat the olive oil then add the meatballs. Cook until the meatballs turn golden brown.

77. Crockpot Mediterranean Chicken Ragù With Orecchiette

Ingredients:
1 + 1/2 cups chicken broth

1 can (14 ounce) petite diced tomatoes

8 artichoke hearts, cut in half

1 roasted red pepper, diced

3 fennel stalks, diced

1 yellow onion, diced

2 tablespoons capers

5 cloves garlic, minced

2 teaspoons dried Italian seasoning

1/4 cup fresh parsley, chopped

1 teaspoon sea salt

1/4 teaspoon black pepper

1 + 1/2 pounds chicken breasts or cutlets, boneless, skinless

8-12 ounces Orecchiette pasta

parmesan cheese, for serving

Directions::
Put in the artichokes, tomatoes, broth, fennel, red pepper, capers, onion and garlic in a 4 quart crockpot. Add and mix in the Italian seasoning then the salt, pepper and parsley.

Cook the chicken breasts on high heat for 4 hours. Remove the chicken then shred using 2 forks. After shredding, put it back in.

In cooking the pasta, follow the instructions or just cook it and make it al dente. Turn the setting to warm and let it set for 10 minutes. Serve the dish with parmesan cheese.

78. Slow Cooker Mediterranean Pork Chops

Ingredients:

¼ cup olive oil

1 cup chicken broth

2 cloves garlic, minced

1 tablespoon paprika

1 tablespoon garlic powder

1 tablespoon poultry seasoning

1 teaspoon dried oregano

1 teaspoon dried basil

4 thick cut boneless pork chops

salt and pepper to taste

Directions:
Combine the garlic, olive oil, chicken broth, paprika, poultry seasoning, garlic powder, basil and oregano in a bowl then whisk.

Put it in the slow cooker.

Meanwhile, cut the pork chop and season it with some salt and pepper. Then, put the pork chops into the slow cooker.

Cover the lid and cook it on low setting for 8 hours.

Pour the sauce and serve.

79. Mediterranean Lentil Soup with Spinach

Ingredients:

1 cup green lentils

1 TBS vegetable oil

2 onions, chopped

2 stalks celery, chopped

2 large carrots, peeled and chopped

1 clove minced garlic

1 tsp. cumin OR 1 tsp. toasted cumin seed, crushed

zest of one lemon

1 potato, peeled and grated

6 cups of vegetable stock

8oz fresh spinach leaves

2 TBS fresh lemon juice

Directions:
1. Put the lentils in colander and rinse using cold water.

2. Meanwhile, cook the carrots, celery and onions for 5 minutes. Add the lemon zest and garlic cumin then cook for 1 minute. Put the transfer mixture to slow cooker. Add the stock, shredded potato and lentils.

3. Cover the lid and cook on low setting for about 8 to 10 hours. Add the lemon juice and the spinach when the vegetables are tender. Cook it on high heat setting for 20 minutes.

80. Slow-Roasted Stuffed Tomatoes

Ingredients:

1/2cup extra-virgin olive oil

3large vine-ripened tomatoes, halved

1 1/2teaspoons salt

1/2teaspoon freshly ground black pepper

3cups fresh bread crumbs

1 1/2cups freshly grated pecorino romano cheese

3cloves garlic, minced

1/4cup finely chopped fresh basil

2tablespoons finely chopped fresh flat-leaf parsley

1/2cup chicken or vegetable broth

Directions
In a 5 to 7 quart slow cooker, pour the ¼ cup ml of the olive oil then put some oil on the side. Add tomatoes in the insert and put some salt and pepper.

Add the cheese, garlic, bread crumbs, basil and parsley in a small bowl. Heap the mixture to every tomato halves and put some olive oil. Put the broth into the slow cooker and cook on high heat for 1 hour. Seam with pan juices. Cover and cook for 1 hour more over high heat. Let tomatoes set for 10 minutes.

Variation: You can also use three 28 to 32 oz. cans of plum tomatoes. Slice the tomatoes in half then put in ¼ cup of extra- virgin olive oil. 2 tbsp. rosemary, 5 minced garlic cloves, 1 tsp. pepper and 2 tsp. salt. Cover the lid and cook on high heat for 1 hour. Sprinkle the tomatoes then cook for 2 hours more on high heat. Take the cover and cook again for 30 minutes more and serve.

81. Slow Cooker Mediterranean Turkey Meatloaf with Roasted Red Potatoes

Ingredients:

1 lb. raw lean white ground turkey

1 tbsp. tomato paste

1/2 cup sundried tomatoes (not packed in oil)

1 large egg

1/4 cup bulgar

2 oz. light feta cheese, crumbled

2 cloves garlic, minced or pressed

1 tbsp. chopped fresh rosemary

1 tbsp. chopped fresh oregano

1 medium baby zucchini, shredded

1 medium red onion, grated

Directions:
1. Spray nonstick cooking spray in the slow cooker.

2. Put all of the ingredients in a bowl. Create a loaf shape in the slow cooker. Cook on low heat setting for 8 to 10 hours. Remove from the slow cooker and allow it to set for 5 minutes.

3. Slice and serve the dish.
Number of Servings: 4

82. Moroccan Turkey with Vegetables

Ingredients:

1 tablespoons olive oil

2 pounds small turkey drumsticks (about 3), patted dry with bottom end removed, if necessary, to fit in slow cooker

1 medium onion, peeled and diced

2 cloves garlic, minced

1 teaspoons ground coriander, plus ½ teaspoon additional at the end

1 teaspoons ground cumin, plus ½ teaspoon additional

1 teaspoon ground cinnamon

1 teaspoon paprika

1 teaspoons ground ginger

2 tablespoons all-purpose flour

1 cup chicken stock, heated

1 cup Coca-Cola (at room temperature)

Pinch salt and freshly ground black pepper

2 small preserved lemons, flesh and seeds removed, and chopped (about 2 ½ tablespoons)

8 ounces baby carrots

1 medium red bell pepper, seeds and membranes removed, diced

1 medium zucchini, sliced

1 can (16-ounce) can chickpeas, rinsed and drained

3 cups pitted small green olives or cut-up large olives

1 cups chopped mint, plus mint leaves to garnish

Directions

TOTAL TIME: 5 hr. 30 min

Prep Time: 45 min

Cook Time: 4 hr. 45 min

In a large skillet, heats the oil then add the drumsticks. Cook the drumsticks on all sides (5 minutes). Put it into the slow cooker.

Put in the onion and cook for about 3 minutes. Add the flour and garlic. Stir and cook for 30 seconds. Add in the ginger, coriander, cumin, paprika and cinnamon. Put in the hot stock and boil the mixture. Add in the Coca-Cola. Stir and put 1 tsp. of black pepper and salt.

Cook on high heat for 15 minutes and simmer. Turn to low heat setting and cook for 3 hours. Put the chickpeas, zucchini, carrots, bell pepper and preserved lemons. Cook for 1 ½ hour

4. Remove the drumsticks from the pot and remove the bones, skin and tendons.

5. Slice the meat in bite-sizes and put it back to the pot. Add mint, cumin, ½ tsp. coriander and green olives.

6. Serve the dish over couscous and garnish some mint leaves.

83. Slow Cooker Tuscan Beef Stew

Ingredients:

1 can (10 3/4 ounces) Campbell's® Condensed Tomato Soup

1 can (10 1/2 ounces) Campbell's® Condensed Beef Broth

1/2 cup burgundy wine or other dry red wine or water

1 teaspoon dried Italian seasoning, crushed

1/2 teaspoon garlic powder

1 can (14.5 ounces) canned diced tomatoes with diced tomatoes with basil, garlic and oregano

3 large carrots, peeled and cut into 1-inch pieces (about 2 cups)

2 pounds beef for stew, cut into 1-inch pieces

2 cans (about 15 ounces each) canned white cannellini beans, rinsed and drained

Directions:
1. In a 3 ½ quart slow cooker, combine the broth, wine, soup, garlic powder, Italian seasoning, carrots, tomatoes and beef.

2. Cover the lid and cook on low heat for 8 to 9 hours.

3. Add the beans and stir. Change the setting to high heat and cook for 10 minutes.

84. Mediterranean braised beef short ribs

Ingredients:

2 tbsp. of vegetable oil

4 lb. beef short ribs, cut into 3- to 4-in lengths, patted dry

4 onions, sliced

1 head of garlic cloves, peeled and halved

796-mL can chopped tomatoes

2 cups of your favorite big red wine

2 bay leaves

1 tbsp. of dried oregano

540-mL can chickpeas

1 cup Kalamata olives, pitted and halved

1 tbsp. drained capers

zest and juice of 1 lemon

1 bunch of parsley, chopped

sprinkle or two of salt

lots of freshly ground pepper

Directions:
1. Set your oven temperature at 300F. Put some oil into the oven and heat it. Cook the beef in batches. Toss in the garlic and onions. Sauté and cook for about 10 minutes.

2. Put the beef into the pot. Add oregano, red wine, bay leaf and tomatoes. Stir and boil.

3. Transfer back to the oven and cook for about 2 to 2 ½ hours. Before serving the dish, add the olives, capers, chickpeas, lemon juice, parsley, lemon zest, pepper and salt.

85. Slow-Cooked Eggplant and Olive Stew

Ingredients:

1 cup chopped onion

1 Tbsp. butter

8 cups chopped eggplant

1 cup pitted kalamata olives

1 Tbsp. minced garlic

1 Tbsp. red wine vinegar, plus 1 Tbsp. extra to taste

700 mL jar of passata (tomato puree)

300 mL water

1 tsp. dried mint

1 tsp. dried Italian seasoning

1 tsp. sea salt (smoked, if possible), plus extra to taste

crumbled organic feta cheese, to serve (optional)

fresh organic oregano, to serve (optional)

Directions:
1. Sauté the onion with the butter in a pot for 5 minutes. Combine the eggplant, stir and cook for 15 minutes.

2. Add water, seasonings, olives, vinegar, garlic and passata. Stir and simmer. Cook on low heat setting for about 45 to 60 minutes.

3. Depending on your taste, you can adjust the seasoning using salt and vinegar.

4. Serve the dish with pasta or rice then sprinkle some feta cheese and oregano.

86. Slow Cooker Chickpea Stew

Ingredients:

3 16-ounce cans chickpeas, rinsed and drained

5 medium carrots, sliced

2 medium potatoes, peeled and chopped

1 cup peeled, seeded, and chopped fresh or canned tomatoes with their juice

1 medium onion, chopped

2 teaspoons chopped fresh rosemary

1/2 cup chicken broth, canned chicken or vegetable broth, or water

2 tablespoons extra-virgin olive oil

Salt and freshly ground pepper to taste

Directions:
Put all of the ingredients in a slow cooker. Cook on low heat setting for 6 to 8 hours. Serve the dish hot.

87. Slow Cooker Italian Chicken with Noodles

Ingredients:

1 1/2 pounds boneless skinless chicken thighs

2 teaspoons dried thyme

1 1/2 teaspoons dried oregano

2 cups chicken broth

1 can (14 1/2 ounces) diced tomatoes, undrained

1 1/2 cups thinly sliced carrots

1 large onion, thinly sliced and separated into rings

3 cups uncooked no yolk egg noodles

3/4 cup frozen peas

Directions:

1. Slice the chicken thigh into 4 pieces and put oregano and thyme.

2. Add the tomatoes, onion slices, carrots and chicken broth in a slow cooker. Put them on top of the chicken. Cover the lid and cook on low heat for about 8 hours.

3. Add the noodles and peas and cook on high heat setting for about 15 to 20 minutes.

88. Greek-Style Gigante Beans

Ingredients:

12 ounces dry gigante beans

1 can (28 ounces) chopped tomatoes, with juice

2 stalks celery, diced

1 onion, diced

4 garlic cloves, minced

Water as needed

Directions:

In a bowl, soak the beans with water for 8 hours. Rinse and drain. Put it into the slow cooker along with the other ingredients. Stir and cook for about 8 to 10 hours.

89. Roast Mediterranean Vegetables And Polenta – A Slow Cooker Recipe

Ingredients:

2 courgettes

1 red pepper

1 yellow pepper

1 aubergine

2 cloves crushed garlic

A carton of baby plum tomatoes

Olive oil

Black pepper

1 tin chopped tomato

1 pack ready-made polenta

Fresh basil leaves

Directions:

1. Chop the vegetables with just the right size.
2. Place all of the vegetables as well as the tomatoes into the slow cooker. Drizzle some olive oil and add crushed garlic and black pepper. Add basil leaves and mix using with your hands.

3. Cook on high heat setting for 2 ½ hours.

4. Before you serve the dish (45 minutes before), put some chopped tomatoes and stir the vegetables.

5. Cut the polenta (1.5 cm thick). Fry it for about 3 to 5 minutes.

6. Serve the dish and enjoy.

90. Braised Mediterranean Chicken

Ingredients:

2 tablespoons olive oil

4to 5 pound chicken, cut up, skin removed

1 teaspoon salt

1/2 teaspoon ground black pepper

3/4 cup white wine, non-alcoholic white wine or cider

1 cup gluten free chicken broth or stock

6 cloves minced garlic

2 teaspoons Herbes de Provence or Italian Seasoning

1 lemon, thinly sliced

1 large red onion, peeled and cut into wedges

1 1/2 cups frozen or canned artichoke hearts, drained and quartered

3/4 cup green olives

Directions:

Heat the oil in a skillet. Use salt and pepper to season the chicken and cook it for about 4 to 6 minutes in a 4 or 5 quart slow cooker.

Pour wine into the skillet and simmer. Remove the bits from the pan. Turn off the heat and add in the garlic, Herbes de Provence and chicken stock. Put the chicken into the slow cooker. Put the lemon slices and onion. Cook on low heat for 4 hours. Add the olives and the artichokes and cook.

Serve the dish with rice or salad.

91. Mediterranean Brisket

Ingredients:

1 (14.5 oz.) can diced tomatoes with juice

1/2 cup dry red wine

5 garlic cloves, chopped

1/3 cup kalamata or other black olives, pitted and chopped

1/2 teaspoon dried rosemary

1 (2 1/2 lb.) piece flat-cut brisket, fat trimmed off

Salt and pepper

1 tablespoon finely chopped fresh parsley

Directions:

1. Put wine, olives, tomatoes and rosemary in a slow cooker and stir. Season meat with 1 ½ tsp. of salt and pepper and put it on top of the mixture. Get half of the tomato mixture and pour it all over the meat. Cover the lid and cook on high heat setting for 5 to 6 hours.

2. Put the brisket to a cutting board and let it stay there for 10 minutes. Remove fat from the sauce then use salt and pepper for seasoning. Cut the brisket and put in a platter. Pour the sauce over the meat and top it with parsley.

92. Mediterranean Beef Ragout

Ingredients:

1/4 c all-purpose flour

1 t dried thyme leaves, crumbled

1 tsp. grated lemon zest, optional 1/2 tsp. salt

1/2 tsp. cracked black peppercorns

2 lbs. trimmed stewing beef, cut into 1-inch cubes

2 Tbsp. olive oil

2 onions, chopped

4 garlic cloves, minced

1 T cumin seeds, toasted

1 cup beef stock 1/2 cup dry red wine

1 can diced tomatoes, including juice

2 bay leaves

2 roasted bell peppers

1/2 cup sliced pitted green olives 1/2 cup finely chopped parsley

Directions:

1. Put the flour, thyme, salt, lemon zest and pepper in a Ziploc bag. Put the beef cubes until everything is coated.

2. Heat 1 tbsp. of olive oil. Cook the beef for 4 minutes and transfer it to the slow cooker.

3. Sauté the garlic and onions. Put the cumin seeds and the flour mixture. Stir for 1 minute.

4. Put wine, beef stock, tomatoes with bay leaf and boil. Cook for a few minutes until it is thickened.

5. Pour the tomato mixture into the slow cooker.

6. Cook on low heat for about 8 hours.

7. About 15 minutes before serving the dish, stir parsley, olives and roasted peppers. Cook on high heat for 15 minutes then remove the bay leaves.

93. Slow Cooker Italian Meatball Stew

Ingredients:

1 dozen Italian Meatballs, click here for Italian Meatball recipe

1 tablespoon olive oil

2 carrots, peeled, chopped

2 stalks celery, coarsely chopped

1 red bell pepper, cored and seeded, diced

1 zucchini, coarsely chopped

1 (14.5 ounce) can fire roasted tomatoes with liquid

1 (15 ounce) can cannellini beans, drained

2 cloves garlic, diced

1 teaspoon dried oregano

2 tablespoons freshly chopped basil or 2 teaspoons dried basil

1/4 teaspoon crushed red pepper flakes

1/2 teaspoon black pepper

Kosher or sea salt to taste

2 cups chicken broth, fat free, low sodium

1/2 cup whole wheat orzo (optional whole wheat couscous or pre-rinsed quinoa)

Directions:
1. In a large skillet, heat the oil and cook the meatballs for about 16 minutes. Add the remaining ingredients except for the orzo. Stir and add the meatballs into the slow cooker. Cook for about 7 to 8 hours on low heat setting.

2. Add the orzo 15 minutes after the cooking time and change the setting to high and cook for 10 to 15 minutes.

3. Serve the dish and put some parmesan cheese.

94. Venison Swiss Steak Mediterranean (Slow Cooker)

Ingredients:

2 cups spaghetti sauce

1/2 teaspoon dried oregano

1 teaspoon salt

1/4 teaspoon pepper

1 3/4 lbs. boneless venison steak, cut to fit crockpot

2 medium onions, cut into chunks

2 cups small whole fresh mushrooms

Directions:
Combine the initial 4 ingredients in a bowl and stir.

Put the steak in a 3 ½ slow cookers and put 1/3 sauce all over the steak pieces.

Sprinkle mushrooms and onions on top of the steak. Put 2/3 of the sauce all over the steak.

Cook on low heat for about 7 to 9 hours.

95. Mediterranean Inspired Shrimp and Sausage Slow Cooker Jambalaya

Ingredients:

1 smoked sausage link, sliced

1 bag jumbo frozen raw shrimp, thawed and peeled

1-1/2 cups white rice

5 strips bacon, cooked and crumbled

1 can tomato puree (29-ounce)

1 can diced tomatoes (14.5-ounce)

1 can pitted black Lindsay Olives (6-ounce), chopped

1 medium onion, chopped

1 clove garlic, minced

1 dried bay leaf

1 tablespoon dried oregano

1 tablespoon dried basil

1 teaspoon garlic salt

1 teaspoon sea salt

½ teaspoon black pepper

1 tablespoon Old Bay seasoning

1 tablespoon Worcestershire sauce

Directions:
In a slow cooker, put the bacon, sausage, diced tomatoes, tomato puree, onion, garlic, olives, oregano, bay leaf, garlic salt, basil, sea salt, pepper, Worcestershire and Old Bay.

Cook over low heat setting for about 5 ½ hours.
Add the shrimp and rice. Stir and turn the heat setting to high. Cover and cook for 30 minutes more.

Serve the dish with olives and garnish with some oregano.

96. Slow Cooker Greek Stuffed Pork Roast

Ingredients:

1 2ish lb. pork roast

2 tsp. olive oil

1/4 cup chopped purple onion

2 cloves of garlic, minced

4 oz. fresh baby spinach

1/4 cup sun dried tomatoes, chopped(I prefer the pouch, not the oil packed)

1 TB fresh parsley, chopped(or 1 tsp. dried)

1 TB fresh oregano, chopped(or 1tsp dried)

1/2 cup feta cheese

1/2 fresh lemon

salt and pepper to taste

Directions:
Soften the sun dried toms with warm water.

Heat oil and sauté garlic and onion.

Add the spinach and wilt down the spinach.

Drain the tomatoes and add it to the skillet together with the parsley and oregano.

Turn off the heat. Add the Feta cheese. Combine and allow it to cool.

Meanwhile, slice the roast lengthwise.

Put the roast into the slow cooker and put the mixture into the roast.

Squeeze ½ lemons on top of the roast

Cook on low heat for about 6 to 8 hours.

Remove from the cooker and let it sit for a few minutes.

Depending on your taste, use salt and pepper for seasoning.

97. Sicilian Pork Stew

Ingredients:

500 g (17.6oz) Pork shoulder (boneless steaks or roasting joint)

1 tbsp. Mild, smoked paprika

1 tbsp. Vegetable oil

50 g (1.8oz) Smoked bacon pieces

150 g (5.3oz) Chorizo, cut into mouth-sized pieces

1 Lemon, quatered

2 tbsp. Lemon juice

3 tbsp. Olive oil

1 handful Black olives

400 g (14.1oz)Chopped tomatoes (tin)

0.5 tsp. Chili flakes, or half a fresh chopped chili

300 g (10.6oz) Butter beans (tin, drained)

150 ml (5.3fl oz.) White wine

350 ml (12.3fl oz.) Water

1 Chicken or pork stock cube

1 pinch Salt

1 pinch Pepper

1 tsp. Dried or fresh sage, chopped

Mediterranean onion base4 Onions, chopped

3 Stick of chopped celery

8 Garlic cloves, chopped

2 tbsp. Olive oil

2 tbsp. Vegetable oil

3 tbsp. Water

Directions:

Set the oven temperature at 375°F/190°C

To create the onion base: Combine all of the ingredients to a covered pan and let it sweat for 15 minutes. Set it aside.

Cut the pork and put some paprika. Heat the vegetable oil and add the pork and bacon. Fry until it gets brown.

Take back the 2 tbsp. onion base to the pan along with the other ingredients and boil. Use salt and pepper for seasoning. Pour it in a huge oven proof dish and cover it foil.

Cook for about 30 minutes then change the temperature to 350F/180C. Cook again for 45 minutes to 1 hour.
Take it out of the oven and put 1 tbsp. of flour on the surface. Put everything into the saucepan and boil to thicken the sauce.

Serve rice or spinach mash.

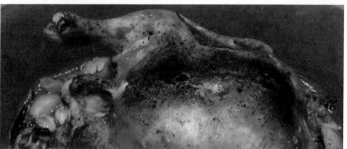

98. Mediterranean Pizza

Ingredients:

160ml (2/3 cup) passata (tomato pasta sauce)

500g pkt Nevana pizza bases

120g coarsely grated mozzarella

100g marinated pitted kalamata olives

100g mushrooms, thinly sliced

1 large yellow capsicum, seeded, thinly sliced

150g pancetta, torn

110g pkt goats' cheese, crumbled

Fresh basil leaves, to serve

Directions:

1. Set the oven temperature at 250ºC and preheat 2 trays in the oven. Put the passata and top it with goats cheese, pancetta, capsicum, mushroom, mozzarella and olives.

2. Bake the pizzas for 10 minutes and garnish with basil leaves.

99. Pot-Roasted Mediterranean Chicken

Ingredients:

3-1/2 lb. whole chicken, rinsed and dried

Sea salt and freshly ground black pepper to taste

2 sprigs fresh marjoram, 10 inches each, leaves stripped

7 sprigs fresh thyme, 4 inches each, leaves stripped

6 medium cloves garlic

5 Tbs. olive oil

1 preserved lemon (or 1 fresh lemon), sliced 1/8-inch thick

7 oz. pitted black olives, such as kalamata

9 oz. button mushrooms

1/2 cup (1-1/2 oz.) sun-dried tomatoes, softened in very

hot water

1 medium onion, cut into eighths

3/4 cup dry white wine

Directions:

Heat the oven at 425°F. Use salt and pepper to season the chicken. With a mini food processor, mix thyme, garlic, marjoram and 1 tbsp. of olive oil to form a paste.

Rub the paste onto the chicken. Put half of the olives, lemon slices and 1/3 of the mushrooms. Drain the sun dried tomatoes and put them all over the chicken. Add the onions and the remaining ingredients (lemon slices, mushrooms and olives). Pour white wine and ¼ cup of olive oil onto the vegetables as well as the chicken. Roast for about 1 to 1 ¼ hours, basting every 10 minutes.

Take the vegetables and put the chicken on a carving board. Remove the trussing and serve the dish with mushrooms, olives, lemons, onions and tomatoes surrounding the chicken.

100. Mediterranean Kale & Cannellini Stew with Farro

Ingredients:

4 cups reduced-sodium chicken broth or reduced-sodium vegetable broth

1 14 1/2 ounce can no-salt-added fire-roasted tomatoes

1 cup farro, rinsed, or kamut

1 cup coarsely chopped onion (1 large)

2 medium carrots, halved lengthwise and thinly sliced crosswise

1 cup coarsely chopped celery (2 stalks)

4 cloves garlic, crushed

1/2 teaspoon crushed red pepper

1/4 teaspoon salt

4 cups coarsely chopped fresh green kale or Swiss chard

1 15 ounce can no-salt-added cannellini beans (white kidney beans), rinsed and drained

3 tablespoons fresh lemon juice

1/2 cup crumbled feta cheese (2 ounces)

Snipped fresh parsley or basil

Directions:

1. In a 3 1/2- or 4-quart slow cooker combine broth, tomatoes, farro, onion, carrots, celery, garlic, crushed red pepper, and salt.

2. Cover and cook on high-heat setting about 2 hours or until farro is tender but still chewy. Stir in kale, beans, and lemon juice. Cover and cook for 1 hour more.

3. To serve, sprinkle each serving with cheese and parsley or basil.

101. Artichoke Pasta

Ingredients:

Nonstick cooking spray

3 14 1/2 ounce cans diced tomatoes with basil, oregano, and garlic

2 14 ounce cans artichoke hearts, drained and quartered

6 cloves garlic, minced

1/2 cup whipping cream

12 ounces dried linguine, fettuccine, or other favorite pasta

Sliced pimiento-stuffed green olives and/or sliced pitted ripe olives (optional)

Crumbled feta cheese or finely shredded Parmesan cheese (optional)

Directions:

Spray a 3 ½ or 4 quart slow cooker with cooking spray.

Drain 2 cans of diced tomatoes. Stir the drained and the other tomatoes, garlic and artichoke hearts.

Cover the dish and cook it on low heat for about 6 to 8 hours. Add and stir the whipping cream and let it stand for 5 minutes.

Cook the paste al dente and drain.

Serve the sauce over the pasta and top with cheese or olives.

CONCLUSION

In combination with moderate exercise and not smoking, this Mediterranean slow cooker dishes offers a scientifically researched, affordable, balanced, and health-promoting lifestyle choice. A true Mediterranean recipe consists mainly of fruits and vegetables, seafood, olive oil, hearty grains, and more—foods that help fight against heart disease, certain cancers, diabetes, and cognitive decline. It's a food worth chasing; making the switch from pepperoni and cheese to fish and avocados may take some effort, but you could soon be on a path to a healthier and longer life. There's no single Mediterranean diet plan, but in general, you'd be eating lots of fruits and vegetables, beans and nuts, healthy grains, fish, olive oil, small amounts of meat and dairy. This lifestyle also encourages daily exercise, sharing meals with others, and enjoying it all. Embracing this is all about making simple but profound changes in the way you eat today, tomorrow, and for the rest of your life. Just as important, these are wonderfully delicious, flavor-filled dishes and meals.

Another plus is using slow cookers which are cheap to buy, economical to use and they're great for making the most of budget ingredients. They offer a healthier, low-fat method of cooking and require the minimum amount of effort.

This collection features delicious and nourishing recipes that evoke the essence of the Mediterranean region while helping you work your way toward optimal health. The robust flavors of Mediterranean cooking are perfect for entertaining, and you don't have to fly all the way to Europe to experience it. Just throw a dinner that will have everyone imagining they're in Italy, Greece, Turkey, or an exotic island in the Mediterranean. Our slideshow of recipes includes classic slow cooker dishes as well as a few new takes. You can make these wonderful dishes to delight your family and friends.

Delicious food that's stood the test of time and helps keep you healthy for years to come. That's at the heart of the traditional Mediterranean cuisine.

Did You Like 101 Mediterranean Slow Cookers?

Before you go, we'd like to say "thank you" for purchasing our book. So a big thanks for downloading this book and reading all the way to the end. Now we'd like ask for a *small* favor. Could you please take a minute or two and leave a review for this book on Amazon

This feedback will help us continue to write the kind of Kindle books that help you get results. And if you loved it, then please let me know

Leave a review for this book on Amazon by searching the title:
Mediterranean Slow Cookers

Or using the QR Code Scanner from your smartphone, scan this code and it will pull up the link directly for you:

Check Out My Other Books

Below you'll find some of my other popular books that are popular on Amazon. Search the titles in Amazon or you can visit my author page on Amazon to see other works done by me.

www.ravenspress.com/jjlewisbooks

Adrenal Reset Diet: 51 Days of Powerful Adrenal Diet Recipes to Cure Adrenal Fatigue, Balance Hormone, Relieve Stress and Lose Weight Naturally

Dukan Diet Explained: The Ultimate Guide to Win the War Against Overweight

Ketogenic Diet: 101 Days of Ketogenic Diet, Low Carb Recipes for Maximum Weight Loss Benefits

12725279R00040

Printed in Poland
by Amazon Fulfillment
Poland Sp. z o.o., Wrocław